gift of Jane Mc Conville
&
Dolores Farrell

THE IMITATION OF CHRIST

THE IMITATION
OF CHRIST

by
THOMAS À KEMPIS

Translated by
RONALD KNOX
and
MICHAEL OAKLEY

Copy 3

SHEED AND WARD - NEW YORK

NIHIL OBSTAT: JOANNES M. T. BARTON, D.D., L.S.S.
CENSOR DEPUTATUS
IMPRIMATUR: E. MORROGH BERNARD
VICARIUS GENERALIS
WESTMONASTERII: DIE XVIII SEPTEMBRIS MCMLIX

The *Nihil obstat* and *Imprimatur* are a declaration that a
book or pamphlet is considered to be free from doctrinal
or moral error. It is not implied that those who have
granted the *Nihil obstat* and *Imprimatur* agree with the
contents, opinions or statements expressed.

First Printing, January, 1960

Second Printing, April, 1960

Library of Congress Catalog Card Number 60–7305

Manufactured in the United States of America

PREFACE[1]

How many books are there whose titles you can clip till they only contain one effective word, and yet be understood by all educated people? The *Apologia* is one, there is Butler's *Analogy*, and Paley's *Evidences*, but you will not find many names to match them: nobody talks of the *Anatomy of Melancholy* as the *Anatomy*, or of the *Origin of Species* as the *Origin*. Such tests are tiny reflectors that give back the glow of fame; and no book passes this test so well as the *Imitation*. Among Catholics at least it is the only book which is mentioned in the same breath with the Bible; among the non-Catholics of yesterday the *Pilgrim's Progress* ("the Pilgrim" for short) was so bracketed. Yet, like other spiritual classics, the *Cloud of Unknowing*, for example, or the *Whole Duty of Man*, it has created problems of authorship. And the reader has a right to expect, here, a dissertation upon the Dutchman, Groote, who is said to have written the first book as it stands, and the degree of recension to which Thomas à Kempis submitted the second and third: with more information about the circumstances in which the work was composed, and the form of it. But this must be omitted, since I am writing away from books—not, however, away from the *Imitation*; it has only once, I think, escaped the packer's eye since I received the subdiaconate. "Do not ask," says Bk. I, ch. 5, "who said this, but listen to what is said." There are no frills about the *Imitation*.

My aim is to seize upon the characteristic method and effect of the book, and I am not sure that this aim has not been already realized when I have said that there are no frills about the *Imitation*. It has the frill-lessness of Euclid and the

[1] This was Mgr. Knox's contribution to "The Catholic Classics" series in *The Tablet* and was first published in the issue of April 20th, 1940. It was written many years before he started to translate the *Imitation* and the quotations from the *Imitation* which appear in it are rendered differently in the present work.

Athanasian Creed. Where the first book is concerned, you
may say that even of the style. "Sometimes we think that
others are fond of our company when in fact it is beginning
to disgust them, from the worthlessness of the character
they see in us" (Bk. I, ch. 8): how could you administer in
less words a cold douche to a man who has spent the evening with friends? "If you cannot make yourself the man you
want to be, how can you expect other people to come up to
your specifications?" (Bk. I, ch. 16): "if you bother so
little about yourself while you are alive, who is going to
bother about you when you are dead?" (Bk. I, ch. 23)—
these are barbs which get beneath the skin of the toughest
among us; and yet how quietly they are shot.

It has been commonly observed that the first book is
concerned almost entirely with the reformation of character,
and a good deal of it might have been drawn from heathen
moralists—in one place, indeed, Seneca is quoted. But if it
was the author's intention to confine himself to the elements
of asceticism, he has certainly outrun his intention; as in the
eleventh chapter, where he writes: "If we were thoroughly
dead to ourselves, and free from attachments within, we
should be able to relish divine things and have some experience of heavenly contemplation". He is already impatient for the illuminative way, and by the first chapter of
Book II he is well into it. Detachment, the conversion of the
regard inwards, the welcoming of mortifications with and for
Christ, are ideals taken for granted. The *Imitation*, wide as
is its use outside the cloister, and indeed outside the Church,
was meant for religious in the first instance, and the author
makes no apology for thus suddenly keying us up to concert
pitch. The rest of Book II is, and is meant to be, "stripping";
we are not to be content with moral suasions, or treat our
own peace of mind as the ideal to be aimed at; we are
concerned with nothing less than the establishment of
Christ's reign in us. If we are ready to give up having our
own way, that is no longer because "it is necessary sometimes to relinquish our own opinion, for the sake of peace"
(Bk. I, ch. 9), but because "you are not to think you have

made any progress until you feel that you are everybody's inferior" (Bk. II, ch. 2). If we avoid gossip, it is no longer because "we rarely return to silence, without finding that we have soiled our consciences" (Bk. I, ch. 10), but because "you will never know interior devotion, until you hold your tongue about what concerns others, and turn back upon yourself" (Bk. II, ch. 5). And learning is to be distrusted as inadequate, not because "he is truly learned, who leaves his own will and does the will of God" (Bk. I, ch. 3), but because "one thing is still wanting . . . that a man should leave all, and leave himself, and go out of himself altogether, and keep nothing for himself of self-love" (Bk. II, ch. 11). We have embarked on an inner circle of spiritual ideas, and no rest is given us. The clerical "we", which softened the effects of Book I, almost disappears in Book II; the author button-holes you with a persistent "thou", and brings every consideration grimly home to you.

So Book II leads us up to that amazingly uncomfortable last chapter, in which the reader feels as if he were being turned over and over on a spit, to make sure that he is being singed with suffering at every point. If a man tells you that he is fond of the *Imitation*, view him with sudden suspicion; he is either a dabbler or a saint. No manual is more pitiless in its exposition of the Christian ideal, less careful to administer consolation by the way. But now, when we feel we have been bullied into the illuminative way, is the stripping part all over? Is the third book to be a collection of maxims illustrating the unitive way, and its glimpses of fruition? Dr. Bigg, in his introduction, writes as if it were: it tells, he says, "of the presence of Christ in the soul, of life in the spirit, of the mystic vision, as à Kempis understood it". This judgement seems to be founded on one or two passages in the third book, rather than on the book as a whole. The twenty-first chapter, that begins with a beating of the wings as the soul aspires towards God, and culminates in the sudden "*Ecce adsum*" of the Divine Lover's intervention, leaves asceticism behind and breathes pure mysticism; but it stands almost alone. The dialogue

7

form of the book—it consists entirely of conversations between Christ and the soul—suggests that it is the fruit of à Kempis' own contemplations; and perhaps the absence of scheme about it can be explained best if we suppose that he simply wrote these down as they came to him in the order of time. But the subjects treated are, for the most part, still in the ascetic sphere; or at best they are consolations addressed to the soul in the dark night which comes before the way of union. It is not in any sense a mystical treatise;[1] the fifty-sixth chapter is still urging us towards the way of the Cross. The writer is still coaxing us onwards; he does not try to take our breath away.

A work without frills—until you reach the fourth book, which is purely a manual for the Communicant, it contains curiously little in the way of theology. The very existence of the Holy Spirit is only recognized, for example, in one or two stray allusions. You can feel the influence of a reaction against the over-subtle speculations of the later medieval theologians; those masters who are more concerned to know than to live well (Bk. I, ch. 3), whose arguments will be silenced when Jerusalem is searched with lamps (Bk. III, ch. 43). A book without frills—was there ever a spiritual author who told us less of his private experiences? It was he, presumably, who felt anxiety about his final perseverance, and was told to act as he would act if he were certain of it (Bk. I, ch. 25); that is the only echo of autobiography. The whole work was meant to be, surely, what it is—a sustained irritant which will preserve us, if it is read faithfully, from sinking back into relaxation: from self-conceit, self-pity, self-love. It offers consolation here and there, but always at the price of fresh exertion, of keeping your head pointing up-stream. Heaven help us if we find easy reading in *The Imitation of Christ*.

R. A. KNOX

---

[1] It is perhaps only fair to state that Mgr. Knox's view of the *Imitation* as "not in any sense a mystical treatise" is not shared by all writers on the mystical life.—*M. O.*

FOREWORD

MONSIGNOR KNOX had for many years before his death made a practice of reading a daily chapter of *The Imitation of Christ*, and it was no matter for surprise that the hand which had given us a masterly new version of the Bible in English should stray towards that time-proved compendium of the spiritual life with which the years had made him increasingly familiar. He had for several years shown a characteristically generous interest in my literary work, whether original or translation, and I was much flattered when in June 1955, after commenting favourably on a version of the *Iliad* I had completed in the style of the original translator, he wrote to me: "If I die without finishing my translation of the *Imitation of Christ*, please tell my executors from me that you are to finish it." I little imagined, when I received this letter, that I should ever be called upon to do so; but only two years later, a bare two months before his death, he wrote in what was to be his last letter to me, "I think I told you I'd instructed Watt [his literary agent] that you were to have the option of finishing off my rendering of the *Imitation*, if I left it unfinished. I'm afraid the present state of my health makes it unlikely that I shall go on with it, and at present it's only reached Bk. II, ch. 4. So don't feel bound to do it if it comes your way; but try your hand if it attracts you. My idea has been to get rid of theological terms (which T. à K. uses rather uncomprehendingly, I think) . . . i.e. I wanted to turn it into a human document." In his last interview with Mr Evelyn Waugh, his literary executor, he expressed the hope that I would finish the translation.

It is as a small token of gratitude for many kindnesses received at his hands—not least among which I reckon the imparting of a little of his matchless skill in writing Latin

9

verse—that I have fulfilled his wish and completed his version in a style of which I hope he would have approved. The Latin text I have used is that of his own shabby and well-used copy, given to him at his ordination, the Dessain text published at Mechlin in 1881 and corrected here and there in his own hand. I have not concerned myself with the niceties of textual criticism, and where the reading is ambiguous I have adopted what seemed to me the more plausible version. For the loan of this volume, whose book-marks include, typically, a photograph of St Thérèse of Lisieux, I am deeply indebted to Lady Helen Asquith, at whose home in Mells Monsignor Knox spent the last years of his earthly life, and in the churchyard beside which his body was laid to rest in 1957.

MICHAEL OAKLEY

20th August, 1959

CONTENTS

	Page
Preface	5
Foreword	9

BOOK I

PRACTICAL ADVICE ABOUT THE SPIRITUAL LIFE

Chapters		*Page*
1.	We must take Christ for our model, and despise the shams of earth	17
2.	On taking a low view of oneself	18
3.	How truth is to be learnt	19
4.	On caution in our undertakings	22
5.	About reading Holy Scripture	23
6.	About immoderate passions	23
7.	About false confidence, and how to get rid of self-conceit	24
8.	On the dangers of too close intimacy	25
9.	On obedience and submissiveness	26
10.	About useless gossiping	27
11.	(a) How to attain peace	28
	(b) About the ambition to do better	28
12.	Why it is good for us not to have everything our own way	30
13.	How temptations are to be kept at bay	31
14.	On avoiding hasty estimates	34
15.	On charity as the motive of our actions	35
16.	On putting up with other people's faults	36
17.	On life in a monastery	37
18.	On the example set us by our holy fathers	38
19.	On the pious practices suitable to a good monk	40

20. (*a*) On the love of solitude and of silence   42
      (*b*) On true and false confidence   43
      (*c*) On the love of one's cell   44
21. About holy sorrow   45
22. A view of man's misery   47
23. On thinking about death   50
24. About the Judgement, and how sinners are punished   53
25. About the zeal we ought to shew in amending the whole course of our lives   56

BOOK II

CONSIDERATIONS INVITING US TO LIVE AN INTERIOR LIFE

1. About living an interior life   60
2. On submitting ourselves humbly to others   63
3. On the character of a peaceable man   64
4. On purity of mind, and singleness of purpose   65
5. On self-criticism   66
6. The satisfaction that comes from having a clear conscience   67
7. On loving Jesus more than anything   69
8. On having Jesus for a close friend   70
9. On lacking all comfort   72
10. On being thankful for God's grace   75
11. On the fewness of those who love the cross of Jesus   76
12. On the royal road of the holy cross   78

BOOK III

ON INWARD CONSOLATION

1. On the way Christ speaks inwardly to the soul   84
2. Truth speaks within us without the outward sound of words   85

CONTENTS

3. We should listen humbly to God's words; many people fail to understand them properly   86

4. We should live humbly and without pretence in the sight of God   88

5. On the wonderful effect of divine love   90

6. On the testing of a true lover   92

7. On concealing grace and making humility its guardian   94

8. On taking a humble view of oneself in God's sight   96

9. Everything is to be seen in its relation to God, our last end   98

10. On the joy of serving God and scorning the world   99

11. On the need to sift and govern the desires of the heart   101

12. On acquiring patience and battling against evil desires   102

13. On humble obedience, after the example of Jesus Christ   104

14. On the need to consider the secret judgements of God; a warning against being vain of our good qualities   105

15. On the way we ought to act and pray with regard to our desires   106

16. True comfort should be sought in God alone   108

17. We must put our whole trust in God   109

18. We must follow Christ in bearing patiently the sorrows of life   110

19. On bearing injuries, and how to tell when you are really patient   111

20. On acknowledging our own weakness and on the miseries of this life   113

21. We must rest in God above all his gifts and favours   114

22. On recalling God's manifold blessings   117

23. On four things that bring great peace   119

24. On avoiding curiosity about the lives of others   121

25. On sure peace of mind and true progress   122

26. On the excellence of a free mind, the reward of humble prayer rather than of reading   123

27. Self-love is a great hindrance in our quest for the highest good   124

28. Against slanderous talk 126

29. How we should call on God and bless him when trouble threatens 127

30. On begging God's help, and being confident of recovering his grace 128

31. On disregarding creatures to find the Creator 130

32. On self-denial and giving up our own desires 132

33. On inconstancy of heart, and directing all we do towards God 133

34. God, above all things and in all things, is the delight of the loving heart 134

35. We are never safe from temptation in this life 136

36. Against the vain judgements of men 137

37. Sincere and utter self-renunciation wins us freedom of heart 138

38. On a good rule of life in outward matters, and on having recourse to God in danger 140

39. A man should not be unreasonably anxious about his affairs 141

40. A man has no goodness of his own, and nothing to boast of 141

41. On despising this world's honours 143

42. Our peace of mind must not depend upon men 144

43. A condemnation of useless and worldly learning 145

44. On not being concerned with outward things 146

45. We should not believe everyone; how easy it is for words to slip out 147

46. On putting our trust in God when others make stinging remarks 149

47. All troubles must be borne for the sake of eternal life 151

48. On the day of eternity and the troubles of this life 153

49. On longing for eternal life, and the joys promised to those who fight to gain that life 155

50. How a man ought to put himself in God's hands in time of trouble 158

51. We should busy ourselves with humble tasks when we fail to reach higher kinds of occupation 161

52. A man ought to think he deserves not consolation but punishment   162

53. God's grace and worldly wisdom do not mix   164

54. On the opposition between the workings of nature and grace   165

55. On the corruption of nature, and the power of God's grace   169

56. We must deny ourselves and follow Christ along the way of the cross   171

57. A man should not be too depressed when he slips into some fault or other   173

58. About God's secrets; we ought not to search into his unfathomable judgements   174

59. All our hope and trust must be placed in God alone   178

BOOK IV

ABOUT THE BLESSED SACRAMENT

A DEVOUT ENCOURAGEMENT TO RECEIVE HOLY COMMUNION

1. On the deep reverence with which Christ is to be received   181

2. On the great goodness and love shewn by God to man in this Sacrament   185

3. On the advantage of frequent Communion   188

4. On the many benefits accorded to those who communicate devoutly   190

5. On the dignity of the Sacrament and on the priestly office   192

6. The question of preparation for Communion   194

7. On examining our conscience and making a purpose of amendment   194

8. On the offering of Christ on the cross, and our own surrender   196

CONTENTS

9. We should offer ourselves and all that is ours to God and pray for all men   197
10. We should not lightly keep away from Holy Communion   199
11. The body of Christ and Holy Scripture are most necessary to the faithful soul   201
12. On the great care we should take in preparing to receive Christ in Holy Communion   204
13. The devout soul should long with heartfelt desire for union with Christ in the Blessed Sacrament   206
14. On the burning desire some devout people have for the Body of Christ   207
15. The grace of devotion is won by humility and self-denial   208
16. We should tell Christ our needs and beg for his grace   210
17. On burning love and eager longing to receive Christ   211
18. A man should not subtly pry into the Blessed Sacrament, but follow Christ, submitting the evidence of his senses to holy faith   213
Index   215

BOOK I

PRACTICAL ADVICE
ABOUT THE SPIRITUAL LIFE

Chapter 1

WE MUST TAKE CHRIST FOR OUR MODEL
AND DESPISE THE SHAMS OF EARTH

He who follows me can never walk in darkness,[1] our Lord
says. Here are words of Christ, words of warning; if we want
to see our way truly, never a trace of blindness left in our
hearts, it is his life, his character, we must take for our
model. Clearly, then, we must make it our chief business to
train our thoughts upon the life of Jesus Christ.

2. Christ's teaching—how it overshadows all the Saints
have to teach us! Could we but master its spirit, what a
store of hidden manna we should find there! How is it that
so many of us can hear the Gospel read out again and again,
with so little emotion? Because they haven't got the spirit
of Christ; that is why. If a man wants to understand Christ's
words fully, and relish the flavour of them, he must be
one who is trying to fashion his whole life on Christ's
model.

3. Talk as learnedly as you will about the doctrine of the
Holy Trinity, it will get you no thanks from the Holy
Trinity if you aren't humble about it. After all, it isn't
learned talk that saves a man or makes a saint of him; only
a life well lived can claim God's friendship. For myself, I
would sooner know what contrition feels like, than how to
define it. Why, if you had the whole of Scripture and all the
maxims of the philosophers at your finger-tips, what would
be the use of it all, without God's love and God's grace?
A shadow's shadow, a world of shadows[2]—nothing matters
except loving God and giving him all your loyalty. And the

[1] John 8. 12. [2] Eccles. 1. 2.

17

height of wisdom is to set your face towards heaven by despising the world.

4. What folly, to hunt for riches that will not last, and put your trust in them! What folly, to set your heart on worldly honours, and scheme for your own advancement! What folly, to obey the promptings of sense, and covet the prizes that will soon cost you dear! What folly, to pray for a long life, without caring whether it is lived well or badly; to think only of your present existence, instead of making provision for the world to come; to fall in love with what passes in a moment, instead of hurrying on to the goal where eternal happiness awaits you!

5. There is one proverb of which we cannot remind ourselves too often, *Eye looks on unsatisfied; ear listens, ill content.*[1] Make up your mind to detach your thoughts from the love of things seen, and let them find their centre in things invisible. Those who follow the call of sense only soil their consciences, and lose the help of God's grace.

Chapter 2

ON TAKING A LOW VIEW OF ONESELF

As for knowledge, it comes natural to all of us to want it; but what can knowledge do for us, without the fear of God? Give me a plain, unpretentious farm-hand, content to serve God; there is more to be made of him than of some conceited University professor who forgets that he has a soul to save, because he is so busy watching the stars. To know yourself—that means feeling your own worthlessness, losing all taste for human praise. If my knowledge embraced the whole of creation, what good would it do me in God's sight? It is by my actions that he will judge me.

2. Why not take a rest from this exaggerated craving for mere knowledge which only has the effect of distracting

[1] Eccles. 1. 8.

18

and deluding us? People are so fond of passing for learned men, and being congratulated on their wisdom—yes, but what a lot of knowledge there is that contributes nothing to our souls' welfare! And there can be no wisdom in spending yourself on pursuits which are not going to promote your chances of salvation. All the talk in the world won't satisfy the soul's needs; nothing but holiness of life will set your mind at rest, nothing but a good conscience will help you to face God unashamed.

3. The wider, the more exact your learning, the more severe will be your judgement, if it has not taught you to live holily. No art, no science should make a man proud of possessing it; such gifts are a terrifying responsibility. Meanwhile, however well satisfied you are with your own skill or intelligence, never forget how much there is that remains unknown to you. Let us have no airs of learning; own up to your ignorance; what is the use of crowing over some rival, when you can point to any number of Doctors and Masters who can beat you at your own game? If you want to learn an art worth knowing, you must set out to be unknown, and to count for nothing.

4. There is no lesson so profound or so useful as this lesson of self-knowledge and of self-contempt. Claim nothing for yourself, think of others kindly and with admiration; that is the height of wisdom, and its masterpiece. Never think yourself better than the next man, however glaring his faults, however grievous his offences; you are in good dispositions now, but how long will they last? Tell yourself, "We are frail, all of us, but none so frail as I".

Chapter 3

HOW TRUTH IS TO BE LEARNT

Oh to be one of those to whom truth communicates itself directly—not by means of symbols and words, whose meaning changes with time, but in its very nature! Our own estimate, our own way of looking at things, is always putting us in the wrong, by taking the short view. And here are we, splitting hairs about all sorts of mysterious problems which do not concern us—we shall not be blamed, at our judgement, for having failed to solve them. Strange creatures that we are, we forget the questions which really matter to us, matter vitally, and concentrate, of set purpose, on what is mere curiosity and waste of time. So clear-sighted we are, and so blind!

2. Why should we be concerned to divide up things into "classes" and "families"? We get away from all this tangle of guess-work, when once the Eternal Word speaks to us. From him alone all creation takes its origin, and therefore all creation has but one voice for us; he, who is its origin, is also its interpreter.[1] Without him, nobody can understand it, or form a true judgement about it. Until all things become One for you, traced to One source and seen in One act of vision, you cannot find anchorage for the heart, or rest calmly in God. O God, you are the truth; unite me to yourself by an act of unfailing love! I am so tired of reading about this and that, being lectured to about this and that, when all that I want, all that I long for, is to be found in you. If only they would hold their tongues, these learned folk! If only the whole of creation would be silent in your presence, and you, you alone, speak to me!

3. Once a man is integrated, once his inner life becomes simplified, all of a piece, he begins to attain a richer and deeper knowledge—quite effortlessly, because the intellectual light he receives comes from above. Freedom of heart is his, and simplicity of intention, and fixity of resolve, and he finds that he is no longer distracted by a variety of occupations; he acts, now, only for God's glory, and does his best to get rid of all self-seeking. There is no worse enemy to your freedom and your peace of mind than the undisciplined affections of your own heart. Really good and holy people plan out beforehand in their minds how they

---

[1] This sentence can be taken in various ways. The last part of it is a quotation from the (inaccurate) Vulgate rendering of John 8. 25.

are to behave in given circumstances; the course of their lives does not sweep them away into following their lower instincts, they shape it for themselves, according to the dictates of right reason. To be sure, the conquest of self demands the hardest struggle of all; but this has got to be our real business in life, the conquest of self—no day passed without beating our own record, without gaining fresh ground.

4. We find no absolute perfection in this world; always there is a background of imperfection behind our achievement; and so it is that our guesses at the truth can never be more than light obscured by shadow. The humble man's knowledge of himself is a surer way to God than any deep researches into truth. No reason why we should quarrel with learning, or with any straightforward pursuit of knowledge; it is all good as far as it goes, and part of God's plan. But always what we should prize most is a clear conscience, and holiness of life. How is is that there are so many people who put knowledge first, instead of conduct? It means that they are constantly at fault, and achieve little— sometimes next to nothing. If only these people would take as much trouble to weed out their imperfections, and to cultivate good qualities, as they take over the learned theses they propound, we should hear less about sins and scandals, less about lax behaviour in religious houses. After all, when the day of judgement comes we shall be examined about what we have done, not about what we have read; whether we have lived conscientiously, not whether we have turned fine phrases. Where are they now, Doctor This and Professor That, whom you used to hear so much about when they were alive, and at the height of their reputation? They have handed over their chairs to other men, who probably never waste a thought on them; while they lived, they counted for something, now they are never mentioned.

5. So soon it passes, our earthly renown. Well for them, if they had practised what they taught; then indeed they would have studied to good purpose. How often the worldly pursuit of useless knowledge brings men to ruin, by dis-

tracting their attention from God's service! They must play the great man, they will not be content with a humble part, and it only leads to frustration. True greatness can only be reckoned in terms of charity; the really great man is one who doesn't think much of himself, and doesn't think much of rank or precedence either. The only clear-sighted man is one who treats all earthly achievements as dirt, because he wants to win Christ; the only educated man is one who has learned to abandon his own will and do God's will instead.

Chapter 4

ON CAUTION IN OUR UNDERTAKINGS

We do wrong to be influenced by every rumour we hear, every suggestion that comes to us; patient care is needed if we are to weigh up the pro's and con's of the business as God sees it. Unfortunately—such is our frailty—people are often ready to believe the worst, instead of the best, about others, and to hand the story on. A fully formed Christian does not believe everything he hears; he realizes how weak human nature is, how bent on mischief, how untrustworthy in its statements.

2. Here is a very wise rule: never act in a hurry, and always be ready to alter your preconceived ideas. And here is another principle that goes with it; don't be too ready to accept the first story that is told you, or hand on to others the rumours you hear, and the secrets entrusted to you.[1] Find out some wise counsellor to advise you, a man of enlightened conscience, and be prepared to go by his better judgement, instead of trusting your own calculations. Believe me, a holy life gives a man the wisdom that reflects God's will, and a wide range of experience. The humbler he is, the more submissive in God's service, the more wise and calm will be his judgements on every question.

[1] "The secrets entrusted to you"; or perhaps, "the opinions you have formed".

Chapter 5

ABOUT READING HOLY SCRIPTURE

It is for truth, not for literary excellence, that we go to Holy Scripture; every passage of it ought to be read in the light of that inspiration which produced it, with an eye to our souls' profit, not to cleverness of argument. A simple book of devotion ought to be as welcome to you as any profound and learned treatise; what does it matter whether the man who wrote it was a man of great literary accomplishments? Do not be put off by his want of reputation; here is truth unadorned, to attract the reader. Your business is with what the man said, not with the man who said it.

2. Mankind is always changing; God's truth stands for ever.[1] And he has many ways of speaking to us, regardless of the human instruments he uses. Often enough, our reading of Holy Scripture is distracted by mere curiosity; we want to seize upon a point and argue about it, when we ought to be quietly passing on. You will get most out of it if you read it with humility, and simplicity, and faith, not concerned to make a name for yourself as a scholar. By all means ask questions, but listen to what holy writers have to tell you; do not find fault with the hard sayings of antiquity—their authors had good reason for writing as they did.

Chapter 6

ABOUT IMMODERATE PASSIONS

Once a man sets his heart on anything immoderately, he loses his peace of mind—the proud man, the avaricious man, how little peace they enjoy! It is the detached, the humble, that live wholly at rest. Strange, how easily a man can be attracted and overcome by some slight, some

[1] *Cf.* Ps. 116. 2.

23

trumpery affection, if he is not yet utterly dead to self! He has no spiritual fibre; nature (you may say) is still strong in him; he has a bias towards the things of sense. And how should he detach himself altogether from worldly desires? Does he leave them ungratified? It is a constant source of irritation to him. Does anybody thwart them? He is ready to fly into a rage.

2. On the other hand, if he gives way to them and gets what he wants, all at once he is struck down by remorse of conscience; that is all that comes of yielding to passion—he is no nearer the peace of mind he aimed at. No, the heart can only find rest by resisting its passions, not by humouring them; heart's rest is for the fervent, the devout, not for the carnally minded, for those who give themselves over to the love of outward things.

Chapter 7

ABOUT FALSE CONFIDENCE, AND HOW TO GET RID OF SELF-CONCEIT

It is nonsense to depend for your happiness on your fellow men, or on created things. What does it matter if you have to be the servant of others, and pass for a poor man in the world's eyes? It is nothing to be ashamed of, if you do it for the love of Jesus Christ. Why all this self-importance? Leave everything to God, and he will make the most of your good intentions.

Put no confidence in the knowledge you have acquired, or in the skill of any human counsellor; rely on God's grace—he brings aid to the humble, and only humiliation to the self-confident.

2. Do not boast of riches, if you happen to possess them, nor about the important friends you have; boast rather of God's friendship—he can give us all we want, and longs to give us something more, himself. Do not give yourself airs

if you have physical strength or beauty; it only takes a spell of illness to waste the one, or mar the other. Do not be self-satisfied about your own skill or cleverness; God is hard to satisfy, and it is from him they come, all these gifts of nature.

3. He reads our thoughts, and he will only think the worse of you, if you think yourself better than other people. Even your good actions must not be a source of pride to you; his judgements are not the same as man's judgements, and what commends you to your fellows is not, often enough, the sort of thing which commends you to him. If you have any good qualities to shew for yourself, credit your neighbour with better qualities still; that is the way to keep humble. No harm, if you think of all the world as your betters; what does do a great deal of harm is to compare yourself favourably to a single living soul. To be humble is to enjoy undisturbed peace of mind, while the proud heart is swept by gusts of envy and resentment.

Chapter 8

ON THE DANGERS OF TOO CLOSE INTIMACY[1]

No need to share your secrets with the world at large; find some man of good sense and piety to be your confidant, and put your difficulties to him. Grudge the time you spend in youthful company, or with strangers from outside. Let us have no flattery of the rich, no fondness for being seen about with important people; humble and simple folk, the pious and the well-disciplined—these are to be your associates, and your talk must be of gracious things. Nor should you be on familiar terms with anybody of the opposite sex; of all good holy women make but one reckoning, and commend them to the mercy of God. Keep your friendship for God and his holy Angels, shunning the acquaintance of men.

[1] Chapters 8 and 9 are meant primarily for religious.

2. Your kindness—everybody has a claim on that; but familiarity has its disadvantages. Sometimes we know a person only by reputation, and that reputation a dazzling one, and then we meet him, and it does not bear looking into. And sometimes, perhaps, when we ourselves imagine that people are enjoying our society, they are really beginning to take a dislike to us, having had time to detect the flaws in our character.

Chapter 9

ON OBEDIENCE AND SUBMISSIVENESS

To stand at your post under obedience, to live at the disposal of a superior, what a blessing it is! How much less dangerous to be obeying orders than to be giving them! And yet there are plenty of people who live under obedience because they have to, not from any love of it; such people find it irksome, and are always ready to complain of their position. Believe me, they will have no sense of freedom until they learn to make a whole-hearted surrender of self for the love of God. Roam about as you will, never will you find rest without humble surrender to the will of a superior. The idea that you can find it by drifting about from one monastery to another is a common one, but it is only a dream.

2. True enough, we all like to have our own way, and we all have a preference for the people whose views agree with our own. But the divine presence is among us; we must aim at peace, and with that aim in view each of us will have to sacrifice, now and again, his own way of thinking. After all, the wisest of us is not omniscient, and it is a pity to be so sure about your own point of view that you never listen to other people's. Quite possibly you are right; but if you forget about that, and let the other man have his way for the love of God, you'll have made the most of the situation.

3. How often I have heard the truth acknowledged, that there is more safety to be found in taking advice than in giving it! A man's judgement may be as sound as you will; but if he cannot bring himself to agree with others when there is good reason, and the nature of the case demands it, it's a sure sign of pride and obstinacy.

Chapter 10

ABOUT USELESS GOSSIPING

Keep clear, as best you may, from the babel of human voices; it is wonderful what distraction is to be found in the discussion of worldly affairs, even when the motive for it is perfectly innocent. Frivolity is infectious, and makes easy prisoners of us. I wish I had kept silence, this many a time, instead of enjoying the society of my fellow men!

What is it that makes us so fond of talking, of gossiping with our friends? We hardly ever come away from it without a guilty conscience. What makes talkers of us, is that we find relaxation, on both sides, in the mere bandying of words; we want an escape from the tedious whirligig of our thoughts. We like giving expression to what is in our minds, especially about the good things we enjoy, or would like to enjoy, and the difficulties we find in our way.

2. And the pity of it is that usually it does no good at all; we may get comfort from finding an outlet like that, but it interferes, more than a little, with that inward comfort which is the gift of God.

We need more watchfulness, more prayer; our time mustn't be frittered away in doing nothing. When you have leave and leisure for talking, let your talk be such as makes for spiritual profit. Victims as we are of bad habit, unambitious as we are about our souls' progress, we speak so unguardedly! And yet there is talk which can be a great spiritual help to us—I mean, the earnest exchange of ideas about spiritual things; especially when two souls, well matched in temper and disposition, find themselves drawn together in God.

Chapter 11(a)[1]

HOW TO ATTAIN PEACE

We could have peace to our hearts' content, if only we would not concern ourselves with the things other people are saying and doing, things which are no business of ours. How can a man expect to have lasting peace when he is always minding other people's business, always looking out for the chance of engaging in external activities, so that recollection is only possible in a small degree, or at rare intervals? Blessed are the simple; they shall have peace to their hearts' content.

Chapter 11(b)

ABOUT THE AMBITION TO DO BETTER

2. We hear of Saints who reached the heights, and became great contemplatives; how did they manage it? They made it their business to wean themselves away from all earthly desires; this left them free to cling, with every fibre of their hearts, to God, and attend to the business of their own souls. We are not like that; we get wrapped up in the objects of our own affections, worried, too, over transitory things; seldom do we conquer a single fault, and the ambition to make daily progress never really kindles us; all is coldness and indifference.

3. If only we could die to self altogether, and enjoy

---

[1] There is no obvious connection between the two halves of this chapter.

complete interior freedom! Then the rest would follow; we should be able to taste the flavours of the spiritual life, and have some experience of what is meant by heavenly contemplation. There is only one obstacle, but it is a formidable one—we have not got rid of passion and desire; we are not really trying to set our feet on the ideal path the Saints trod. When we encounter even the slightest degree of difficulty, we are all too ready to turn, in despair, to human consolations.

4. And yet, if we would only play the man, and stand our ground, depend upon it, we should find heaven coming to our aid. As long as they rely on his grace, God is always ready to help people who put up a fight; he only gives us the opportunity of fighting because he wants us to win.

You are careful about the external observances of religion? Yes, but if we identify our souls' progress with things like that, we shall soon come to the end of our spiritual resources. We have to apply the axe to the root of our natures, and clear our passions away, before we can attain to peace of mind.

5. If we could manage to eradicate one of our faults every year, how soon it would make perfect men of us! As things are, it is just the other way round; we often feel that our lives were better, and more free from taint, when we first turned to God than they are now, after all these years spent in religion. Our eagerness, our sense of achievement, ought to be growing intenser every day; and here we are, treating it as something remarkable when some poor remains of that early enthusiasm are still left to us!

If we would only put constraint on ourselves, just a little, at the very beginning! The rest would follow, simply and cheerfully enough.

6. Oh, it is not easy, saying good-bye to the ways we have got accustomed to, but it is much easier than a frontal attack on the will; and if you cannot win the day in light skirmishes, what success can you expect when it comes to the really difficult part? You must begin by saying No to your inclinations, getting out of bad habits, or they will

29

involve you in worse trouble as time goes on. If you could but realize what a difference it makes, a life well lived, the peace of mind it would bring you, the encouragement it would give to others! I can't help thinking you would be more deeply concerned about your progress in the spiritual life.

Chapter 12

WHY IT IS GOOD FOR US
NOT TO HAVE EVERYTHING OUR OWN WAY

It's good for you to go through difficult times now and again, and to have your will thwarted; the effect is often to make a man think—make him realize that he is living in exile, and it is no use relying upon any earthly support. It's good for you sometimes to hear men's voices raised against you, and to find that you are making a bad impression, or at least a false impression, on others, even when you are doing your best, and with the best intentions. It often makes for humility; prevents you from having too good an opinion of yourself. It's when we make a bad surface impression, and people are ready to think ill of us, that we learn to fall back upon God's judgements, because he witnesses all our actions from within.

2. And that is what we are aiming at; a man ought to rely so firmly on God that he has no need to be always looking about for human support.

A good Christian man[1] can derive profit from the afflictions, the temptations, the unhallowed thoughts which assail him. At such times, he realizes more than ever his need of God; he becomes conscious that no power for good lies in him, apart from divine grace. He falls to prayer, sighing and groaning over the misery he endures, tired, now,

---

[1] Literally "A man of good will". In Luke 2. 14, this phrase almost certainly means "men upon whom God looks with favour". But it is sometimes understood to mean "men in good dispositions".

of life itself, and wishing that death might come, so that he could lose himself, and be with Christ. No better warning could be given him that in this world neither true freedom of mind nor true peace is to be found.

Chapter 13

HOW TEMPTATIONS ARE TO BE KEPT AT BAY

As long as our life here lasts, we shall never be rid of difficulties and temptations; that is why the book of Job tells us that man's life on earth is one long probation. Each one of us, then, has his own temptations, calling for special care; he must pray over them and be on the watch against them, or the devil is sure to find an opportunity of taking him unawares—the devil, our unsleeping enemy, who roams about continually, looking for his prey.[1] Nobody can reach to such heights of sanctity that he is never tempted; there is no such thing as being above temptation altogether.

2. These temptations can be a wearisome burden to a man, but none the less of great use; they humiliate him, and purify him, and teach him wisdom. Trials and temptations —these have always been the stepping-stones by which the Saints marched forward; only those who failed at the test forfeited their chances, and fell back.

Nowhere will you find a monastery so enclosed, or a hermitage so remote, that temptation and difficulty cannot follow you there.

3. Never, as long as he lives, can a man tell himself that he is beyond the reach of temptations; we are sinners born, and the focus of them lies in ourselves. When one of them leaves us, another comes instead; there will always be trials for us to endure—have we not lost the gift of happiness? People often try to run away from temptation, only to find that they are plunged in it deeper than ever; you can't win

[1] Cf. 1 Peter 5. 8.

a battle by simply running away. You need patience and humility, if you want to rise superior to all your enemies.

4. The man who is content with a mere mechanical avoidance of his faults will make little headway; all at once the temptations will come and make themselves felt more acutely than before. Believe me, patience and endurance, with God's grace to aid them, will bring you better success in the end than any violence, any frantic efforts on your own part.

When temptation comes, the oftener you take advice about it the better. And when others ask for your advice in this way, do not treat them harshly; ply them with words of comfort, such as you would wish to hear if you were in their case.

5. When we are tempted to do wrong, the root of the trouble is always the same—fickleness of mind, and want of trust in God. A ship without a rudder, how easily the waves drive it this way and that! So it is with the man who has grown slack, and lost his sense of aim; you never know what he will be tempted to do next.

Temptation, to elect souls, is what the fire is to iron; it tests their quality. Often enough, our capacities are greater than we know, and it is only when we are tempted that our true nature appears. All the same, we ought to be careful about temptation, especially in its early stages; easier to dispose of your enemy, if you never let him set foot within the gateway of the mind, but meet him outside, on the threshold, the moment he knocks. One of the poets has a tag about it:

"Check the first fault; too late the medicine's brewed
    When poisons rage inveterate in the blood".

That is how it is with us; at first it is a mere thought confronting the mind; then imagination paints it in stronger colours; only after that do we take pleasure in it, and the will makes a false move, and we give our assent. It is all so gradual, this wholesale infiltration of our malignant enemy; and all because we put up no resistance at the start. The longer they last, these sluggish reactions of ours, the feebler a man's resistance grows from day to day, and the enemy's assault more powerful.

6. Are these temptations fiercest when the soul first turns to God, or in the later stages of its advance? It differs with different people; and there are some who have a rough passage, you may say, all through their lives, while the tests to which others are subjected are gentle enough. It is all part of God's design for us, so wise, so just, always taking into account the circumstances of each man's life and the merit of his actions, with the salvation of the elect as the end of it.

7. No reason, then, for despair when we find ourselves exposed to temptation; it only means that we must pray to God more earnestly than ever, asking for his gracious help in all our trials. Has not St. Paul told us that God, with the temptation itself, will ordain the issue of it, and enable us to hold our own?

Humbly, then, let us submit to God's dealings with us, when any temptation or trial comes; it is the humble soul he will set free, and lift up to greatness.

8. No such test as these of a man's spiritual progress, no such occasion of merit, no such arena to shew his fighting qualities. After all, when a man is not conscious of any difficulties in his path, is it any special credit to him to be devout and zealous? But let him carry himself patiently when everything goes against him—then there is good promise of spiritual advancement.

Why is it that some people are preserved from grave temptation, yet fight a losing battle all the time against their petty, day-to-day faults? Surely it is to keep them humble; with such proof of their frailty in things of little moment, they are not likely to err through self-confidence where great issues are at stake.

Chapter 14

ON AVOIDING HASTY ESTIMATES

Watch your own step; be slow to criticize the doings of other people. When we criticize others, we get nothing for our pains; how often we make mistakes! How carelessly it can lead us into sin! Be your own critic; pull yourself to pieces; then you will have something to shew for your trouble. Again and again our judgement about a thing depends on the way our sympathies are engaged; a personal preference can easily rob us of the power to see straight. This obstinacy in our own opinions would have less power to disturb our judgements, if all the desire of our hearts found its only scope in God.

2. But too often some hidden force within, some attraction that meets us from outside, will sweep us off our feet. Plenty of people are influenced in their actions by these undercurrents of self-seeking, without having any idea of it. All seems to go well with them, as long as everything turns out in accordance with their wishes, their plans; but when once their wills are thwarted, they lose their balance and get depressed in no time.

3. Disputes will always be arising, even between friends and fellow citizens, even among religious and devout souls, about differences of policy or opinion; men are slow to give up old customs, reluctant to be led on farther than they can see. And if you depend on your own reasoning and research, not on the overmastering influence of Jesus Christ, will they get enlightened counsel from you? Seldom, and with difficulty. God wants us to submit wholly to his mastery and to outsoar human reason by the fervency of our love.

Chapter 15

ON CHARITY AS THE MOTIVE OF OUR ACTIONS

Nothing in the world, no love of any human creature, ever justifies us in doing what is wrong; but there are times when a man well employed is free to put aside his task, or to employ himself better still, at the call of another's need. In that case, the good he planned does not come to nothing; it is transformed into something better.

The performance of an action is worthless in itself, if it is not done out of charity. Charity must be our motive; then everything we do, however little and insignificant, bears a rich harvest. After all, what God takes into account is not so much the thing we do, as the love that went to the doing of it.

2. It was a great thing you did, if great love did it; well done is greatly done. Act for the public good, not for your own pleasure; then you act well.

But, too often, the motive we mistake for charity ought rather to be described as a merely human motive. How hard it is to banish those other motives—natural propensity, self-will, the hope of getting something in return, an eye to our own advantage!

3. Whereas true charity, charity that goes the whole way, leaves no room for self-seeking; it is God's glory that must have, everywhere, the preference. A man who has charity of that kind does not envy other people; how should he, when he cares nothing for selfish pleasures? Not for him the joys that are centred in self; in God, high above all earthly good, he finds his hope of blessedness. How should he think of " good " as belonging to any human creature? He ascribes the possession of it to God alone; to God, the Source from which all things flow, the End in which the Saints, all of them, attain fruition and repose.

Oh for a spark of real charity! That would be enough to make a man realize the hollowness of all earthly things.

Chapter 16

ON PUTTING UP WITH OTHER PEOPLE'S FAULTS

There will always be faults in ourselves, faults in others, which defy correction; there is nothing for it but to put up with them, till God arranges things differently. After all, it may be the best possible way of testing your patience; and without patience a man's good qualities go for very little. At the same time, you do well to pray about such inconveniences; ask God in his mercy to help you bear them calmly.

2. If you have spoken to a man once and again without bringing him to a better mind, it is a mistake to go on nagging at him; leave it all in God's hands; let his will be done, his name be glorified, in the lives of all his servants— he knows how to bring good out of evil.

Yes, you do well to cultivate patience in putting up with the shortcomings, the various disabilities of other people; only think how much they have to put up with in you! When you make such a failure of organizing your own life, how can you expect everybody else to come up to your own standards?

3. We like to have everybody around us quite perfect, but our own faults—we never seem to correct *them*. Tom, Dick and Harry must be strictly called to order, but we aren't fond of being called to order ourselves. It is always the other man that has too much rope given him—our wishes must not be thwarted; rules for everybody else, but our own liberties must not be abridged for a moment. My neighbour as myself—it is not often, is it, that we weight the scales equally?

If we were all perfect, we should give one another no crosses to bear, and that is not what God wants.

4. He will have us learn to bear the burden of one another's faults. Nobody is faultless; each has his own burden to bear, without the strength or the wit to carry it by himself; and we have got to support one another, con-

sole, help, correct, advise one another, each in his turn.

Meanwhile, there is no better test of a man's quality than when he cannot have things his own way. The occasions of sin do not overpower us, they only prove our worth.

Chapter 17

ON LIFE IN A MONASTERY

There is a great deal to be done by way of breaking yourself in, if you mean to preserve peace and harmony when you are living in community. To enter a monastery or a congregation, live there without reproach, and be true to your vocation till death—all that is a serious undertaking; no greater happiness than to live a holy life in a cell, and make a good end. But do you mean to hold your own, and get the best out of it? Then you must carry yourself like an exile that has no home in this world. You must be Christ's fool, if you want to live the life of a religious.

2. To take the habit, to get the tonsure, does not carry you far; what makes you a real religious is the changing of your life, is dying completely to your own inclinations. If you came here looking for something that wasn't just God and the salvation of your soul, you mustn't expect to find anything but trouble of mind and unhappiness.

Another thing—you will be a disturbing influence before long, unless you make up your mind to take the lowest place, and be at everybody's disposal.

3. You came here to obey orders, not to issue them. A vocation means having a hard time and doing honest work, not loitering about and gossiping. This place is meant to test people, like the furnace in which you assay gold; and only one thing will help you to stand up to the test—wholehearted self-abasement for the love of God.

Chapter 18

ON THE EXAMPLE SET US BY OUR HOLY FATHERS

Look at our fathers in the old days, living masterpieces as they are and shining examples of true religion; and see how feeble our own achievement is, almost nothing. Heaven help us, what is our life in comparison with theirs? Holy people these, true friends of Christ, that could go hungry and thirsty in God's service; cold and ill-clad, worn out with labours and vigils and fasting, with praying and meditating on holy things, with all the persecutions and insults they endured.

2. Apostles and Martyrs, Confessors and Virgins, and all those others who would follow in Christ's footsteps, many and grievous were the trials they went through, caring nothing for life in this world, if life might be theirs in eternity.

And then, the holy fathers in the desert—how severe that life was, how full of self-renunciation! The long periods of searching trial, the devil's constant assaults; prayer offered to God so frequently and so fervently, and stern fasts kept; all that burning ambition to rise higher in the spiritual life, that gallant campaign to overcome their faults; the clear eyes, the true wills, that aspired towards God! After a day of hard work, they must still be long over their praying—as if work itself had meant rest, for a moment, from mental prayer!

3. Never a minute of the day but was spent profitably, never an hour but seemed too short to give them time enough for God; so sweet was the taste of contemplation, they would forget that their bodies needed food as well. Riches, titles, honours, their friends, their families—they would say good-bye to all that; nothing of the world must be left to them. Of food, they would scarcely take enough to support life itself; they had to attend to their bodily needs sometimes, but they grudged the necessity. So poor they were in the things of this world, so rich in graces and vir-

tues; poor men outwardly, but inwardly refreshed by grace, and its heavenly consolations.

4. Strangers to the world? Yes, but close friends, intimate friends of God. How he loved them, how he treasured their love, these men who thought themselves good for nothing, these men whom the world despised! Kept steady by sincere humility, unquestioning obedience their rule of life, charity and patience to guide them—that was how they advanced, day by day, in the spiritual life, and won such graces with God. Why don't we imitate these people, we religious, take up their challenge and go forward, instead of following the unadventurous herd, and growing slack?

5. Only think, how fervent were all the religious orders, at the time when their holy institutes were first established! They prayed so devoutly, they set their hearts on holiness of living; strict discipline reigned, and all was reverence and obedience, that flourished under the old Master's Rule.[1] Records enough survive to shew us what kind of men they were; men of real holiness, trained to perfection, that could fight valiantly, and tread the world down under their feet.

Nowadays, if we come across somebody who keeps the rules, somebody who can bear his lot with patience, we think the world of him.

6. What a half-hearted, careless state we must have fallen into, that we should have lost, so soon, our early enthusiasm; that we should be tired out, lukewarm, weary of life itself! Never be it said that you fell asleep over your task of growth in holiness, you, who have had all these examples of devotion constantly before your eyes.

[1] The phrase used in the original, *sub regula magistra* looks like a direct allusion to the very early monastic document called "The Rule of the Master" (*cf.* the Abbot of Westminster in the *Ampleforth Journal* of May, 1950). The rendering sometimes given, "under the control of a Superior", cannot be got out of the Latin.

Chapter 19

ON THE PIOUS PRACTICES SUITABLE TO A GOOD MONK

The life of a good monk must be full of gracious qualities; he ought to be, inwardly, what he looks like outwardly. And indeed, there should be much more in him than meets human eyes; it is really God who is watching us, so that we ought to be abashed by his presence. Should we not be pure as angels, when we walk, like the Angels, in his sight?

As each new day comes, we ought to renew our good resolutions, re-kindle the fires of our devotion, as if today were the first day of our coming back to God. "Help me, Lord God," we ought to say to him, "in carrying out my good resolutions, in this holy business of serving you. Help me, today, to make an effective start; so far, I have really nothing to shew for it."

2. Progress means a programme; with the best will in the world, it is an anxious business, and if the man who has a firm resolve often fails to keep it, what of the man who seldom or never makes any fixed resolution at all? Those resolutions—what a lot of excuses we find for breaking them! Even a minor omission, where these pieties of ours are concerned, doesn't go unavenged; there is always loss somewhere. That is why holy people, when they make a resolution, depend more on God's grace than on any wisdom of their own; in all their decisions, it is the grace of God that gives them confidence. They know that "man proposes, and God disposes"; the course of a man's life is not what he makes it.

3. To be sure, you will have to omit a pious custom, now and again, because some work of mercy, or some service to your brethren, calls you away; in such a case, you will find no difficulty in taking it up again. But if you give it up from mere *ennui* or mere negligence, you are definitely at fault, and you will feel the ill effects of it.

Try as we may, we shall still be betrayed into a number of

shortcomings; but it is useful none the less to have a resolution about something definite, and concerned especially with the faults that are the greatest hindrance to our progress. Outward behaviour, inward thoughts, should alike come up for review, should alike be regulated; both of them have much to say to our spiritual progress.

4. If you can't be in a state of recollection all the time, at least you should collect your thoughts at intervals; at the very least once a day, every morning, let us say, or every evening. Morning is the time for making resolutions; when evening comes, analyse your past behaviour—what sort of person have you been today? What have you said, or done; what have been your thoughts? In any of these ways, you may have offended God and your neighbour oftener than you knew.

Take your coat off, and stand up like a man to the devil's treacherous assault. Restrain your appetite for food, and you will find it easier to restrain all your bodily appetites. Never leave your time quite unoccupied; always be either reading, or writing, or praying, or meditating, or doing work of some kind for the benefit of the community. But, when it comes to bodily mortifications, these should be practised with discretion; they are not meant for everybody alike.

5. Your practices of devotion, when they do not take the form of community exercises, must not be for all the world to see; being your own private affair, they had best be performed in secret. And, at the same time, don't let yourself grow slack over community exercises, and hurry on to your own. Carry out, fully and faithfully, the obligations enjoined on you; and then, if you have time left over, you can be your own master, using what devotions you will.

You can't expect everybody to use the same practices of piety; one suits you and another suits me. What is more, different ones appeal to us as more suitable to different occasions. Some we like more on feast-days, others are for daily use; some we need more in times of difficulty, others when all is calm and quiet; some chime in best with our melancholy moods, others with those moments when we rejoice in the divine consolation.

6. When the great feasts come round, our pieties must take on a fresh lease, and we must ask the Saints for their help more urgently than ever. Always our good resolutions should look forward from one feast to the next, as if that was the date on which we were to leave this world for a better, and keep, there, eternal holiday. In this way, the holy seasons will call for careful preparation; for special holiness of life and a specially strict observance of all our duties. Only a short time now, we shall feel, before God calls us to enjoy the reward of the work we have done for him.

7. And if that moment is delayed, let us rest assured that it was because we were not ready for it; we are not worthy, as yet, of that glory which will make itself known in us when the appointed time comes. We must make a point of being better prepared, next time, for the move. *Blessed is that servant*, we read in St. Luke, *who is found watching when his Lord comes; I promise you, he will give him charge of all his goods.*[1]

Chapter 20(a)

ON THE LOVE OF SOLITUDE AND OF SILENCE

You must find time somehow for cultivating your own society; God's mercies to you need a lot of thinking over. At such times, put your thirst for knowledge on one side; read so as to soften the heart, not so as to divert the mind. Must you be always gossiping, always going about aimlessly, picking up the latest rumours? If you can do without that, you will find plenty of suitable occasions for getting on with your meditation. The great Saints always avoided the society of other people as much as they could; they wanted to be alone, waiting upon God.

[1] Luke 12. 43, 44.

2. And what does the old tag say? "I never yet went out among men, without feeling less of a man when I came home."[1] How often we have that experience, at the end of a long chat! Easier to keep your mouth shut than to talk without saying too much; easier to bury yourself away at home than to watch your step successfully in public. If you are really aiming at an interior life, a spiritual life, you must be off with Jesus, away from the crowd.

Chapter 20(b)

ON TRUE AND FALSE CONFIDENCE[2]

Never trust yourself to appear in public, unless you love solitude; to speak, unless you love silence; to come to the front, unless you would sooner be at the back; to give orders, unless you know how to obey them.

3. And never trust your own feelings of light-heartedness, unless you are sure that they have a good conscience behind them. The confidence of the Saints—that is a different matter; it was always permeated with the fear of God. All those good qualities, all those dazzling graces, didn't for a moment make them less anxious or less humble about themselves. Whereas the confidence sinners feel comes from pride and presumption, and it is going to let them down in the end. You may pass for a good monk or a good hermit, but you must never think yourself secure, as long as this life lasts.

4. It is not uncommon for the people who stand highest in the world's estimation to be in the greatest danger—they are too sure of themselves. Indeed, for many of us it is a good thing that we should not be wholly free from temptation; its frequent assaults keep us on the watch, so that we are less likely to grow conceited, and perhaps allow ourselves too much liberty in the pursuit of earthly comfort.

[1] Seneca's Letters, No. 7.
[2] This section is a parenthesis, not directly connected with what precedes, or with what follows.

Chapter 20(c)

ON THE LOVE OF ONE'S CELL

No more hunting for momentary pleasures, no more entangling ourselves with the world, and what a clear conscience we might have! What peace, what calm we might enjoy, if we would cut out all useless preoccupations, and think only about our salvation, only about divine things; if we would make God the unique centre of our hopes!

5. If a man would earn heavenly consolations, he must school himself carefully in the discipline of holy sorrow; and if that sorrow is to be heart-felt, you must go back to your cell, and shut it tight against the noises of the world. Scripture tells you as much: *In your bed-chambers feel the sting of sorrow.*[1] You will find it waiting for you in your cell, the thing you have so often looked for in vain outside it.

A cell lived in is a cell loved; little frequented, it will get on your nerves. Be a good tenant, a good caretaker to it, when you first enter religion, and you will find it a cherished friend, a welcome consolation, later on.

6. It is in silence and in repose that the devout Christian makes progress; the hidden truths of Scripture are revealed to him, and so, night after night, he finds himself bathed in salutary tears. The further from the world's din, the more intimacy with the world's Creator; if you want God and his Angels to draw near, you must keep friends and cronies at a distance. Hide yourself away with an eye to your soul's welfare; that will do you more good than to go about doing miracles, with your own needs forgotten.

It is a good sign in a religious if he seldom goes out, if he shuns appearing in public, and is disinclined for human company.

7. Why do you stand looking in at the shop window, when you can't go inside? The world and its gratifications pass away. Always the lure of the senses will be tempting us to take a stroll abroad, but what is left after a brief hour

---

[1] This is a translation of the inaccurate Vulgate rendering of Ps. 4. 5.

of enjoyment? All you carry home with you is a troubled conscience, and a distracted mind. Glad journey out, sad journey home; a gay night means a grey morning; how often that is true! How insidiously they creep in, the pleasures of sense, yet lead to nothing but remorse and ruin!

8. All you could see elsewhere, you can see just as well here; sky and earth and the four elements—that is all the stuff the world is made of; and all you see anywhere will only last a little while, here under the sun. You dream of fruition, but the dream is unattainable; if the whole of our transitory existence could pass before your eyes, it would be nothing but an empty show. Look heavenwards, look Godwards; ask pardon for what you have done, and left undone. Idle thoughts for idle minds; only one thing claims your attention, God's will for you.

Shut yourself in, and call the well-loved presence of Jesus to your side; let him share your cell with you; nowhere else will you find such peace. Why did you ever leave it? Why did you listen to all that gossip? You would have done better to preserve your peace of mind; so eager, yesterday, to hear the latest news, you bear the burden of troubled thoughts today.

Chapter 21

ABOUT HOLY SORROW

If you want to make any progress, the fear of God must be always about you: don't expect to be wholly free from restraint. You will have to keep all your senses under control, instead of giving yourself up to thoughtless enjoyment. Indulge, rather, your heart's sorrow; that way lies devotion. A sorrowing heart is the key to so many blessings which a wasted hour can easily fritter away! It's surprising, isn't it, that man's heart can ever be really contented in this life, when he reflects seriously on his exiled state, on the many dangers his soul runs?

2. Frivolity of mind, and carelessness about our faults, deaden us to the sense of our souls' misery; and so, as often as not, we find ourselves giving way to empty laughter, when there is good reason for tears. There can be no real freedom, no enjoyment worth having, unless the fear of God, and a good conscience, goes with it.

Well for you, if you can manage to clear all distractions out of the way, and concentrate on a single point—the exercise of holy sorrow. Well for you, if you can say good-bye to all that leaves a stain behind it, and burdens the conscience. Strive hard to reach that goal; habit must be formed, if habit is to be overcome. People will not let you go your own way? Yes, they will, if you leave them to go theirs.

3. Don't make other people's business your business; watch your own step all the time, and don't waste all your good advice on your friends; keep the best of it for yourself.

No need to be depressed, if you find that your fellow men don't think much of you; what ought to be weighing on your mind is that you are not behaving like a true servant of God, like a good religious—that is where you need to improve, to be more on the watch. Quite often we shall find it does us more good, and involves less risk, if we don't get much comfort out of this life, especially where human comfort is concerned. If we get little or no supernatural comfort either, that is our own fault;[1] we haven't set our hearts on holy sorrow, and so we don't go the whole way in renouncing the paltry enjoyments of sense.

4. As for supernatural comfort, be sure you have done nothing to deserve it; affliction, and plenty of it, is all you deserve.

Once a man is master of this craft of sorrow, how full of weariness and bitterness the whole world seems to him! Look where he will, a good Christian man finds much to

[1] This statement must be accepted with reservation. Most spiritual writers teach that the lack of "consolations" is a test of our faith, not the punishment of infidelity.

make him weep for sorrow; whether he looks into his own heart, or looks round at other people, he soon realizes that there's no such thing in this world as a life free from trouble. And the more carefully he looks into his own heart, the more deeply will he feel it; after all, what are the real grounds for our regret, for this inward sorrow? Our sins, those vicious habits of ours, that hardly ever let us think about heavenly things, so completely are we wrapped up in them.

5. If you thought more about death, and less about the years that lie ahead of you, you couldn't help being more eager to amend your life. And again, if you reflected seriously on the punishments that await you, whether in hell or in purgatory, I feel certain you would be more ready to put up with difficulty and suffering; no hardship would have any terrors for you. But there it is—these things don't get in under the skin; we are still in love with the allurements of sense; that's why there's no fire in us, no energy.

6. Often, when our wretched bodies are quick to complain, the trouble is weakness of the spirit.

Pray to the Lord humbly, then, for this gift of sorrow; say, in the words of the sacred author, *Lord, allot me for food, for drink, only the full measure of my tears.*[1]

Chapter 22

A VIEW OF MAN'S MISERY

Wretched you needs must be, wherever you are and wherever you turn, unless you turn to God. Why make all this to-do about thwarted wishes, and blighted hopes? Was there ever man that got his own way all the time? Of course not, neither you nor I nor anybody else in the world—everybody has some troubles, some difficulties to put up with, kings and Popes like the rest of us. And who comes off best? The

[1] Ps. 79. 6.

man who can stand up to a certain amount of suffering for the love of God.

2. Plenty of people can't—weak, flabby natures, that are always complaining, "Look at So-and-so; what a good time he has! How rich, how important he is; what influence and rank he enjoys!" But in reality, if you take one look at the prizes of heaven, you will see that all these earthly ones count for nothing; if anything, it is a weight on our minds, the precarious possession of them, a constant source of anxiety and alarm. Man's happiness doesn't consist in having more earthly possessions than he knows what to do with; a moderate fortune is all he needs.

A life of wretchedness, that's what our life on earth is. The higher a man's spiritual aims, the more distasteful does our present life appear to him; he sees more clearly, feels more deeply, the disabilities of our fallen nature. He must eat and drink, sleep and wake, labour and rest—all these natural needs have their claim on him, and it makes a devout soul feel wretched and harassed; why can't he be clear of it all, beyond the reach of sin? Do you doubt that bodily needs are a heavy burden to the spiritual man? Then why does the sacred author pray so earnestly to be delivered from them—*Lord, deliver me from my needs*?[1]

But it will go hard with the people who don't realize their own wretchedness; harder still with those who are in love with this wretched, perishable life. There are people who so cling to it, even when they can scarcely support it by hard work, or on charity, that they would never give the kingdom of God a thought, if they had the chance of living here endlessly.

4. Minds without sense, hearts without faith! So deeply rooted in earth's soil, they have no appetite but for material things. Alas, when their end comes, these people will be wretched still! Then they will begin to realize how worthless and how unreal were the things they loved on earth. Whereas God's Saints, and all that were true friends of Christ, have always been indifferent to what gratified nature,

[1] Ps. 24. 17.

to the hopes that bloomed so fair on earth; all their hope, all the set of their minds, aspired to the joys that are eternal. Upward it went, the whole longing of their hearts, to reach the abiding things, the things that are not seen; there should be no love of things seen, to drag them down to the depths.

No need, brother, to lose heart about your spiritual progress; time and opportunity are still yours.

5. Why postpone your good resolutions? Up with you, and set about it this instant; tell yourself, "Now is the time for action; this is zero-hour, just the right moment for making something better of my life". But you are feeling low, and finding things difficult? Why, that is the very opportunity you want, to win your spurs! Of course you must pass through fire and water, before you can reach the cool shade. Put constraint on yourself, or never a fault will you overcome.

This body of ours is a weak instrument; so long as we carry it about with us, we have not said good-bye to sin, and we have not said good-bye to fatigue and unhappiness either. All very well, to wish we could be eased of our wretchedness, but thére it is—by sinning, we have lost our innocence, and all true happiness with it. Patience, then, patience; we must wait for God's mercy to relieve us; wait till the curse is lifted, and our mortal nature is swallowed up in life.

6. What a feeble thing is this human nature of ours, always ready to slip down-hill! The sin you commit today is the same sin you mentioned yesterday in confession; an hour has gone by, and those resolutions about avoiding it might just as well not have been made. Haven't we good reason to feel ashamed? Can we ever entertain a good opinion of ourselves, weak and wavering creatures as we are? A moment's carelessness, and we have lost ground—the ground grace had won for us after such long, such painful struggles!

7. So early in the day, and already we are taking it easy! What state shall we be left in, at the day's end? Heaven help us, if we propose to turn in and take a rest, as if all were

49

quiet and safe, when our life doesn't, even now, shew a single trace of genuine holiness! It would do us no harm at all if we could go back to the innocent days of our novitiate, and start training for perfection all over again; in that way, at least, we might hope to mend our ways for the future, and make more advance than we do at present in the ways of the spirit.

Chapter 23

ON THINKING ABOUT DEATH

Your time here is short, very short; take another look at the way in which you spend it. Here man is today; tomorrow, he is lost to view; and once a man is out of sight, it's not long before he passes out of mind. How dull they are, how obdurate, these hearts of ours, always occupied with the present, instead of looking ahead to what lies before us! Every action of yours, every thought, should be those of a man who expects to die before the day is out. Death would have no great terrors for you if you had a quiet conscience, would it? Then why not keep clear of sin, instead of running away from death? If you aren't fit to face death today, it's very unlikely you will be by tomorrow; besides, tomorrow is an uncertain quantity; you have no guarantee that there will be any tomorrow—for you.

2. What's the use of having a long life, if there's so little improvement to shew for it? Improvement? Unfortunately it happens, only too often, that the longer we live the more we add to our guilt. If only we could point to one day in our life here that was really well spent! Years have passed by since we turned to God; and how little can we shew, many of us, in the way of solid results! Fear death if you will, but don't forget that long life may have greater dangers for you.

Well for you, if you keep an eye on your death-bed all the time, and put yourself in the right dispositions for death as each day passes. Perhaps, before now, you've seen a man die? Remember, then, that you have got the same road to travel.

3. Each morning, imagine to yourself that you won't last till evening; and when night comes, don't make bold to promise yourself a new day. Be ready for it all the time; so live, that death cannot take you unawares.

Plenty of people die quite suddenly, without any warning; the Son of Man will appear just when we are not expecting him. And when that last hour comes, you'll find yourself taking a completely different view of the life that lies behind you. How bitterly you will regret all that carelessness, all that slackening of effort!

4. If you hope to live well and wisely, try to be, here and now, the man you would want to be on your death-bed. What will give you confidence then—the confidence which ensures a happy death? To have despised the world utterly; to have longed earnestly for advancement in holiness; to have loved discipline, to have taken penance seriously, to have obeyed readily, to have renounced self, to have put up with everything that was uncongenial to you for the love of Christ.

You see, there is so much you can undertake while you are still in health—what will you be able to manage, when illness comes? Illness doesn't often change people for the better, any more than going on pilgrimage makes saints of them.

5. You will have friends and relations to pray for you? Don't, for that reason, leave the business of your soul to be settled later on.[1] You will be forgotten sooner than you imagine; better make provision now, by opening a credit account for yourself, than trust to the good offices of other people. You, so unconcerned about yourself today—why should other people concern themselves about you to-morrow? No, here is the time of pardon; the day of sal-

---

[1] "The business of your soul"; literally, "your salvation". But this might be taken to imply that our prayers can win the salvation of a soul which has died in mortal sin; a conclusion which would be false to Catholic theology. The warning given here appeals to the fear of purgatory, not to the fear of hell.

vation has come already. The more pity you should make so little use of it, your opportunity for winning a title to eternal life. Some time, you'll know what it is to wish you had another day, even another hour, to put your life straight; and will you get it? There's no saying.

6. My friend, my very dear friend, only think what dangers you can avoid, what anxieties you can escape, if you will be anxious *now*, sensitive *now* to the thought of death! Make it your business so to live, today, that you can meet death with a smile, not with a shudder, when it comes. If that moment is to be the beginning of a life with Christ, you must learn, now, to die to the world; if you are to find free access to Christ then, you must learn now to despise everything else. A body chastened by mortification means a soul that can face death with sure confidence.

7. Poor fool, what makes you promise yourself a long life, when there is not a day of it that goes by in security? Again and again, people who looked forward to a long life have been caught out over it, called away quite unexpectedly from this bodily existence. Nothing commoner than to be told, in the course of conversation, how such a man was stabbed, such a man was drowned; how one fell from a height and broke his neck, another never rose from table, another never finished his game of dice. Fire and sword, plague and murderous attack, it is always the same thing—death is the common end that awaits us all, and life can pass suddenly, like a shadow when the sun goes in.

8. Once you are dead, how many people will remember you, or say prayers for you? To work, friend, to work, as best you may, since there is no saying when death will come, or what will be the issue of it. Hoard up, while there is still time, the riches that will last eternally; never a thought but for your soul's welfare, never a care but for God's honour. Make yourself friends now, by reverencing God's Saints and following their example; when your tenancy of this life is up, it is they who can give you the freehold of eternity. Live in this world like some stranger from abroad, dismissing its affairs as no concern of yours; keep your heart free,

and trained up towards God in heaven—you have no lasting citizenship here. Heaven must be the home you long for daily, with prayers and sighs and tears, if your soul, after death, is to find a happy passage to its Master's presence.

Chapter 24

ABOUT THE JUDGEMENT,
AND HOW SINNERS ARE PUNISHED

At every turn of your life, keep the end in view; remember that you will have to stand before a strict Judge, who knows everything, who cannot be won over by gifts or talked round by excuses, who will give you your deserts. What sort of defence will you make before One who knows the worst that can be said against you—poor, sinful fool, so often panic-stricken when you meet with human disapproval! Strange, that you should look forward so little to the Day of Judgement, when there will be no counsel to plead for you, because everyone will be hard put to it to maintain his own cause! Now is the time to work, while there is a harvest to be reaped, now is the time when tears and sighs and lamenting of yours will be taken into account, and listened to, and can make satisfaction for the debt you owe.

2. Nothing so important, nothing so useful, if you want to clear your soul of that debt, as to be a man who can put up with a great deal. Such a man, if he is wronged, is more distressed over the sin committed than over the wrong done him; he is always ready to say a prayer for his enemies, forgives an injury with all his heart, and is quick to ask forgiveness of others, and you will find him more easily moved to pity than to anger. And all the while he is putting constraint upon himself, doing all he can to make corrupt nature the servant of the spirit.

Much better to get rid of your sins now, prune away your bad habits here, than keep them to be paid for hereafter;

it's only our preposterous attachment to creature comforts that blinds us.

3. Those fires, what is it they will feed on but your sins? The more you spare yourself, and take corrupt nature for your guide, the heavier price you will pay later on, the more fuel you are storing up for those fires. The pattern of a man's sins will be the pattern of his punishment; red-hot goads to spur on the idle, cruel hunger and thirst to torment the glutton; see where the dissipated souls, that so loved their own pleasures, are bathed in hot pitch and reeking sulphur, where the envious souls go howling like mad dogs, for very grief!

4. Each darling sin will find its appropriate reward; for the proud, every kind of humiliation, for the covetous, the pinch of grinding poverty. Spend a hundred years of penance here on earth, it would be no match for one hour of that punishment. Here we have intervals of rest, and our friends can comfort us; there is no respite for the damned, no consolation for the damned.

Take your sins seriously *now*, be sorry for them *now*, and at the Day of Judgement you will have confidence, the confidence of blessed souls. How fearlessly, then, the just will confront those persecutors of theirs, who kept them down all the time! The man who submitted to human judgements so meekly will now take rank as judge; in perfect calm they will stand there, the poor, the humble, while the proud are daunted by every prospect that meets them.

5. We shall see, then, what the true wisdom was—learning how to be a fool, and despised, for the love of Christ; troubles endured with patience will be a grateful memory to us, and it will be the turn of the wicked to look foolish. See how all pious souls make merry, and the scoffers go sad; how the body that was mortified shews fairer, now, than if it had been continually pampered; how rags are all the wear, and fine clothes look shabby; how the gilded palace shrinks into insignificance beside the poor man's cottage! The dogged patience you shewed here will do you more good than all earth's crowns; you will get more credit

for unthinking obedience than for any worldly wisdom.

6. Philosophy will be less consolation to you than a good clean conscience, and all the treasures on earth won't outweigh the contempt of riches. The devout prayers you offered, not the good meals you ate, will be your comfort then. The silence you kept, not the long chats you had, will be pleasant to think of then. Saintly deeds done, not phrases neatly turned, will avail you then. A well-disciplined life of hard penitential exercise, not a good time here on earth, will be your choice then.

You have got to realize that all your sufferings here are slight ones,[1] and will get you off much worse sufferings hereafter. How much will you be able to stand there? The amount you can stand here is a good test. You, who find it so hard to bear these pin-pricks, how will you be able to take eternal punishment? What will you make of hell, when you make such a to-do about small discomforts?

No, you can't have your own way twice over; you can't take your pleasure in this world and then reign with Christ.

7. And now, suppose you had lived all your life, and were still living today, surrounded with honours and pleasures, what use would it all be, if you were to fall down dead this instant? Everything, you see, is just meaningless, except loving God and giving all our loyalty to him.

Love God with all your heart, and you've nothing to fear; death or punishment, judgement or hell; love, when it reaches its full growth, is an unfailing passport to God's presence. If we are still hankering after our sinful habits, of course we are afraid of death and judgement. Just as well, all the same, that if love can't succeed in beckoning us away from evil courses, we should be scared away by the fear of hell. Only, if a man doesn't make the fear of God[2] his first consideration, his good resolutions won't last; he will walk into some trap of the devil's before long.

---

[1] Many editors render "Learn how to suffer just a little here", but this does not translate the Latin.

[2] The author appears to be contrasting the (filial) fear of God with the (servile) fear of hell. But it is tempting to suppose that he wrote "fear of God" inadvertently instead of "love of God", which would give a much better sense to the passage.

Chapter 25

ABOUT THE ZEAL WE OUGHT TO SHEW IN AMENDING THE WHOLE COURSE OF OUR LIVES

You have to watch carefully and work hard, if you are to serve God. Ask yourself, all the time, what you came here for; why it was that you left the world behind you. The idea was, surely, that you should live only for God, and become a man of prayer. Set your heart, then, on making progress; it will not be long before the reward of your labours is granted you—no fears, no regrets after that, to invade your peace. Only a little effort is demanded of you now, and deep repose shall be yours; nay, eternal happiness. If you keep faith with God, by working busily, never doubt that he will keep faith with you, by rewarding you generously. Always cherish a well-grounded hope of attaining the prize, but don't let it make you careless—that will lead to slackness and self-conceit.

2. There was a man once, who was all fears at one moment, and all hopes the next. And at last a day came when he threw himself down before one of the altars, and thus gave expression to the thoughts in his mind, "If I only *knew* that I was going to persevere!" And all at once he heard the divine answer in his heart, "Well, and if you did? What line of action would you propose to take? If you take that line of action now, you will feel cheerful enough." Consoled by these words, he took heart, and resigned himself to God's will, and so all his troubles and flutterings came to an end. Gone those anguished speculations about the future; all he wanted to know about was God's will, so satisfying, so perfect in its design—the only real motive for starting out on any holy purpose, or going through with it.

3. *Trust in the Lord's mercies, and do what is right; cultivate the piece of ground he has given you, and all its riches shall be yours.*[1]

[1] Ps. 36. 3.

So many people are kept back from spiritual growth, and from tackling their faults in earnest, by one single fault— running away from difficulties; we don't like a tussle. And the plain fact is that the people who get ahead of their neighbours in the fight for spiritual advancement are precisely the people who launch an attack just where the going is difficult, just where everything seems against them. Conquest of self, inward mortification—that's what wins you ground, that's what earns you fresh grace.

4. True enough, in the race for self-conquest we don't all start with the same handicap; but a man of strong passions, if he really tries hard, will be able to make more progress than a man of orderly habits, who is less ambitious for holiness. For a real amendment of life, you need two things above all—you must wean yourself away from the faults to which your nature is specially prone, and you must press on hard in pursuit of the good quality you most need.

Habits to be avoided, or corrected—the ones you are always criticizing in other people.

5. You see, there's profit to be derived everywhere; when you see or hear about some good example, you can imitate it, when you notice some habit that deserves censure, you can avoid it—or, if you've already got into it yourself, be at pains to correct it as soon as possible. Meanwhile, if you've a good eye for other people's faults, don't forget that they're watching you.

How it does one good to come across a community that is really zealous, really devout; where the life is well ordered, and the rule is kept! And what sight is so mournful, so depressing, as the go-as-you-please community, in which the work it was called to do gets left undone? Such a lot of harm is done by the people who lose sight of the intention for which they were founded, and divert their energies[1] to what is no business of theirs.

6. Remind yourself of the undertaking to which you are committed, and then go and look at your Crucifix. You've

---

[1] "Divert their energies" is very doubtful Latin. It seems possible that the author wrote "gradually turn aside" (a difference of only one letter in the Latin).

good reason to be ashamed, haven't you, when you think of the life Jesus Christ lived—all these years in religion, and so little attempt, even now, to make him your model! If he meditates on the holy life and Passion of our Lord, any religious can find there all that he needs, and more than he needs, for his soul's profit; he won't want to look for better subjects elsewhere. Jesus crucified! If only we could get that into our hearts, all the learning we need would be ours in no time.

7. Lay what commands you will upon a religious who has his heart in it, he can stand anything, manage anything, easily enough. But a religious who has grown slack, and lost interest, is tormented both ways; no escape for him to right or left; he has no solace for his weariness within, and he's not allowed to look for it outside. A religious living beyond the reach of discipline is exposed to grave perils. The man who is always looking for relaxations of the rule will always be in difficulties; rebellious when they are refused, dissatisfied when he gets them.[1]

8. What kind of life is it they lead, all those other religious, who are strictly bound to the discipline of the cloister? They seldom go out, they live retired, eat most sparingly, dress rough, work much, talk little, watch late, rise early, still at their prayers, still at their books, hedging themselves in all round with observance. See how the Carthusians, the Cistercians, and many other orders of men and women rise each night and sing their praises to God! Shame on you, that you should lie abed at this sacred hour, when such a multitude of religious are just setting about their carolling.

9. How wonderful it would be if we had no duties at all, except to lift up heart and voice in praise of our Lord God! If you never needed to eat or drink or sleep, so that you could go on praising God, with no leisure but for holy employment! How much happier you would be than you are now, forced one way and another to look after your

---

[1] "Rebellious when they are refused, dissatisfied when he gets them"; this seems the best interpretation of the unenlightening phrase, "for either one thing or the remaining thing will displease him".

bodily needs! What a pity that we should *have* needs of this kind; should need anything except that spiritual refreshment which the soul tastes, but tastes, alas, too seldom.

10. It's not till a man reaches the stage of refusing consolation from any created thing, that he gets his first real taste of God. By that time, he has learned to be content, however things fall out; he won't be elated by big results, or disappointed with small ones. In utter confidence he takes his stand upon God, who is everything to him in every connection; the God for whom nothing is ever lost, nothing ever perishes—to whom everything is alive, obeying, instantly, the least expression of his will.

11. Keep on reminding yourself that life comes to an end, and lost time never returns to us. You aren't going to form any good habits without taking trouble over it, working hard for it. The moment you begin to cool off, trouble starts. You must throw yourself into it whole-heartedly; then you will experience great peace of mind, and all your labour will seem light; God's grace and the love of holy living will carry you along. Meanwhile, there's more hard work in it, this fight against your bad habits and your passions, than in the sweat of bodily exertion. The man who doesn't keep clear of petty faults will gradually slip into graver ones. A day spent profitably means an evening spent cheerfully. Watch yourself, spur yourself on, check yourself with a warning now and again; whatever claims other people have on you, don't let your own soul suffer from neglect. The more constraint you put on yourself, the more progress you will make; that is certain.

BOOK II

CONSIDERATIONS INVITING US
TO LIVE AN INTERIOR LIFE

Chapter 1

ABOUT LIVING AN INTERIOR LIFE

God's kingdom lies within you, the Lord says.[1] You must turn to him, the Lord, with all your heart, and leave this wretched world behind you, if your soul is to find rest. Learn to despise this world of outward things, and devote yourself to what lies within; there, within you, you will see the coming of God's kingdom. That's what "God's kingdom" means—peacefulness and rejoicing in the Holy Spirit; something denied to the irreligious. Christ is ready to come to you, with what kindness in his glance! But you must make room, deep in your heart, to entertain him as he deserves; it is for the inward eye, all the splendour and beauty of him; deep in your heart is where he likes to be. Where he finds a man whose thoughts go deep, he is a frequent visitor; such pleasant converse, such welcome words of comfort, such deep repose, such intimate friendship, are well-nigh past belief.

2. Up with you, then, faithful soul, get your heart ready for the coming of this true Lover, or he will never consent to come and make his dwelling in you; that is his own way of putting it, *If a man has any love for me, he will be true to my word; and we will come to him, and make our abode with him.*[2] You must make room for Christ, then, and shut the door upon all intruders.

If Christ is yours, then wealth is yours; he satisfies all your wants. He will look after you, manage all your affairs for you most dutifully; you will need no human support to rely on. Our human friends change so easily, fail us after

[1] Luke 17. 21.   [2] John 14. 23.

such a short time! Whereas Christ abides for ever, and stands loyally, to the last, at our side.

3. A human friend, that shares our frail mortality, may do us good service and endear himself to us, but it is a mistake to repose much confidence in him. Why should we make such a tragedy of it if he takes the wrong side now and again, in opposition to us? Friends today, enemies tomorrow, and the other way round—it's always the same; men's hearts veer like the breeze. Put all your trust in God; centre in him all your fear and all your love; he will make himself responsible for you, and all will go well as he sees best.

This world is no native country of yours; go where you will, you are only a foreigner, only a visitor in it. Nothing will ever bring you rest, except being closely united to Jesus.

4. Why stand gaping here? This is no place for you to settle down. Heaven is your destination, and you should look upon this earthly scene only as a transit-camp. Transient, all created things, and you as much as the rest of them; cling to them, and you will get caught up in them, and be lost. All your thoughts must be at home with God, all your prayer make its way up to Christ continually.

Ah, but it is above your reach (you complain), such high contemplation of heavenly things. Why then, let your mind come to rest in Christ's Passion, and find in his sacred wounds the home it longs for. Take refuge in those wounds, those precious scars, as a devout soul should, and you will feel, in all your troubles, a deep sense of consolation. How little you will care for the contempt of your fellow men, how easily you will put up with their criticisms!

5. When Christ lived in the world, he too met with human contempt; his own intimate friends, at the hour of his greatest need, left him to face insult. Christ so ready to suffer and be despised, and have you complaints to make? Christ with enemies and slanderers all about him, and do you expect to find nothing but friendship and kindness? The crown is for endurance; where is it going to come from,

if you never meet with difficulties? If you want to have everything your own way, you are no friend of Christ's; you must hold out with him, and for love of him, before you can share his kingdom.

6. If you'd ever really got inside the mind of Jesus, ever had a single taste of his burning love, considerations of your own loss or gain would mean nothing to you; you would be glad to have insults heaped on you—the love of Jesus fills us with self-contempt.

If you love Jesus, if you love the truth, if you really direct your gaze inwards, and rid yourself of uncontrolled affections, then you can turn to God at will, lifted out of yourself by an impulse of the spirit, and rest in him contentedly.

7. The man who can experience all the values of life, not judging them by what's said about them, or the price that's put upon them, but as they really are—he is the true expert; his learning is not human but divine. And a man like that, who knows how to walk by the light within him, and make little account of outward things, doesn't have to look for a suitable place, or wait for a suitable time, before he falls to his devotions. Living in this inner world, he never squanders his attention on the things of sense, and recollection comes easy to him. Is there practical work to be done? Some business that can't be put off? He doesn't feel it as an obstacle; he is adaptable enough to take things as they come.

If there's order and discipline in your own soul, the doings of other people won't surprise you or put you out.

8. If you are fond of interfering, to that extent you will always be faced with difficulties and distractions; if you were all right in yourself, if you'd really been through the process of purification, you'd be able to turn anything to good account, and profit by it. Why is it that such a lot of things get on your nerves, and are always disturbing your peace of mind? Because you've never really died to self, never really weaned yourself away from earthly things. The unchastened love of creatures—that's what disfigures and

entangles a man's conscience as nothing else does. If you refuse all outward consolation, heaven will come into your view, and fill you, again and again, with spiritual rejoicing.

Chapter 2

ON SUBMITTING OURSELVES HUMBLY TO OTHERS

Don't think it a matter of great importance whether So-and-so agrees with you or disagrees with you; act in such a way as to make sure, whatever you are doing, that God is on your side. As long as you have a clear conscience, God will keep you clear of harm; human malice can't touch you, if the divine aid is forthcoming. Not a doubt of it, if you will make up your mind to suffer in silence, you will find that he comes to your aid; he knows just when and how to bring you deliverance; you have only to put yourself in his hands. How you are to get out of this or that difficulty, this or that embarrassing situation, is God's business, not yours. After all, what harm can it do, other people knowing about your weaknesses and taxing you with them? Often it's the best possible thing for you; it helps to keep you humble.

2. If a man will only be humble about his own short-comings, how little it takes to disarm ill-feeling, how little it costs to put things right! It's humble people God protects and preserves, God loves and comforts; he stoops down and gives his grace lavishly, raising the humble man to heights of glory, as soon as neglect has done its work. Such a man he chooses for his confidant, beckons to him gently and calls him apart. Only a humble man takes it calmly when he is put to the blush; what does it matter? It is God, not the world, that gives him countenance. Never think that you have made any progress, till you have learned to regard all men as your betters.

63

Chapter 3

ON THE CHARACTER OF A PEACEABLE MAN

Peace in your own soul first of all, then you can think about making peace between other people. Peaceable folk do more good than learned folk do. When a man is at the mercy of his own feelings, he misinterprets the most innocent actions, always ready to believe the worst; whereas your peaceable man sees good everywhere; at peace in himself, he isn't suspicious of others. It's when you become discontented and unbalanced that your mind is torn by suspicions; there is no rest for you, no rest for those around you. You are always saying the wrong thing, and missing your chance of doing the right thing; you are jealous about your rights, and forget that you have duties. If you will begin by having a high standard yourself, you can afford to have a high standard for other people.

2. How is it that you are so glib in excusing yourself, putting a good colour on your own actions, and won't listen when excuses are offered to you? Honesty should make you accuse yourself, excuse your neighbour; bear with him, when you expect him to bear so much from you. Believe me, you've got a long way to go before you can lay claim to real charity, real humility. There should be only one target for all this angry resentment—yourself.

You get on well with gentle, good-natured folk? Why, so does everybody; we all like to have friends around us, we all have a soft spot for the man who agrees with us. But when people are difficult and cross-grained, when they get out of hand and keep on contradicting us, to keep on good terms with *them*—ah, that needs a lot of grace; that's a man's job, and you can't praise it too highly.

3. People differ so; there are contented people, ready to live contentedly with others; and there are restless people, who give no rest to those around them, a burden to others and a worse burden to themselves; and there are those who restrain their own passions, and do their best to restrain the

passions of others. But in this imperfect life, when all's said and done, peace doesn't mean having no enemies, it means being ready to put up with ill-treatment. It's the man who has learnt the craft of suffering who really enjoys peace. He is his own master, and the world lies at his feet; he has Christ for his friend, and heaven for his patrimony.

Chapter 4

ON PURITY OF MIND, AND SINGLENESS OF PURPOSE

There are two wings that lift a man from the ground, singleness of heart and purity; the one regulates your intentions, the other your affections. The single-hearted man makes for God; the pure-minded man finds and enjoys him. No right course of action will have difficulties for you,[1] if only you're free in your own heart, free from ill-regulated desires. Such freedom will only come to you in full measure when you've made God's will and your neighbour's good your sole aim, your sole consideration.

If the dispositions of your heart were really true, everything in the world would be a mirror reflecting eternity, a book to teach you heavenly wisdom. After all, there's no creature in the world so mean and insignificant that it doesn't reflect, somehow, the glory of God.

2. You'd see everything with clear eyes, fit everything into the pattern of your thought, if goodness and purity were at the roots of your being. The pure heart has a range of vision that can reach the heights of heaven, the depths of hell. It's what he is in himself that determines a man's judgement of what lies outside himself. If there is such a thing as enjoyment in this world, it's an innocent mind that has the key to it; and if there is real misery and frustration to be found anywhere, go to the man with a bad conscience —he will tell you about it.

[1] Literally, "will hinder (or entangle) you", a difficult phrase which it is hard to illustrate from the author's use of language elsewhere.

Put a bar of iron in the fire, and all the rust disappears; there's nothing but a uniform white glow. And so it is when a man turns right round towards God; the indifference flakes off him, and you've got a new man to deal with.

3. The moment you begin to lose interest, how formidable is the least effort! How gladly you distract your mind with worldly things! Whereas the moment you tackle the business of self-conquest thoroughly, and trudge manfully along the path of God's will, you make no account of the difficulties that seemed, till now, insurmountable.

Chapter 5

ON SELF-CRITICISM

We aren't in a position to count on ourselves much, because apart from a rare grace, we haven't enough perception; our faculty of insight is a very limited one, and is easily lost if we once get careless about it. Quite often we're unaware of our own blindness, and make a bad action worse by the dishonest excuses we offer for it—we lose our tempers, for example, and put it down to zeal, or we pounce on slight faults in our neighbours so as to have an excuse for ignoring more serious faults of our own. How quick we are to reckon up our grievances against other people, how slow to notice what a lot they have to put up with from us! And yet a man who sees himself as he really is hasn't the heart to criticize the next man.

2. It's a sure sign that you're living an interior life, if in your own view you are Problem number One; something which has to be tackled seriously, so that you don't feel inclined to discuss other people. Don't gossip about their affairs, be content to watch yourself, or you'll never be a man of prayer and recollection.

God and yourself—that's the subject to keep in view; mere outward happenings oughtn't to make much impres-

sion on you. How your thoughts roam about when you're
not recollected; how little ground they've covered when
you haven't kept yourself in view! No, if you really want
peace, really want to be integrated, you must leave everything else on one side, and keep one thing under observation
—yourself.

3. The passing shows of time, how you grow in stature
if you can banish these from your thoughts, how they
belittle you if you pay attention to them! Let nothing impress
or overawe you, nothing charm or captivate you, except
God and what comes straight from God; the satisfaction
you get out of creatures must count for nothing. The soul
that loves God despises everything else, as being less than
God; he only, the Eternal, the Infinite, can fulfil every desire,
can bring balm to the soul's wounds, and true joy to man's
heart.

Chapter 6

THE SATISFACTION THAT COMES
FROM HAVING A CLEAR CONSCIENCE

There's only one kind of record a good Christian man
thinks worth having, and that's the record of a clear conscience. With a clear conscience, you can be happy all the
time, you can put up with any amount of ill treatment, and
smile at any misfortune; it's the burdened conscience that
is always full of alarms, never at rest. Nothing can disturb
your calm, if your heart feels no twinge of remorse; nothing
ought to cheer your spirits, except knowing that you've done
your duty. Of course, the evil liver can have the illusion of
happiness, but it's only an illusion, there's no peace of mind
there really; *for the rebellious*, God says, *there is no peace.*[1]
"We're all right," these people say, "no harm can befall
us; who's going to have the courage to do us an injury?"

[1] Isaias 48. 22.

But don't be taken in by that; God's vengeance, you'll see, will overtake them suddenly, and all they did will be undone, all their plans will come to nothing.

2. It isn't difficult for a man who loves God to congratulate himself on the sufferings he has to undergo; that's what's meant by "making a display of the Cross of Jesus Christ". How short-lived, by comparison, are the congratulations men exchange between themselves! And indeed, there's always a kind of melancholy attaching to the glory we attain in this world; so that, as we were saying, the only record a good Christian values is the record of his own conscience, not any testimonial paid him by his fellow men. He wants to win the glory that will last for ever, and he can't get up much enthusiasm about our brief, earthly reputations. To go about hunting for that kind of reputation, and indeed to treat it with anything but contempt, means that you haven't really set your heart on the glories of heaven.

Oh, what peace of mind it brings us, being indifferent to other people's praise or criticism!

3. What restful content we enjoy, as long as we have the approval of our own consciences! After all, nobody's praise is going to make a saint of you, and nobody's abuse is going to make a villain of you; you are just what you are, the thing God sees in you—there's no going beyond that. What matters is what you're really like in yourself; concentrate on that, and the gossip that's talked about you will have no interest for you. Men see but outward appearances, God reads the heart, in the sense that men only watch one another's actions, whereas God weighs up the motives from which we act.

To act always for the best, and yet to have a low opinion of yourself, is the test of a humble soul; and if you can do that without human support, that's fresh proof of a pure intention, and an intimate trust in God.

4. But to make sure that you've put yourself entirely into his hands, you want one thing more—you must be quite indifferent to the approval of your fellow men. As St. Paul

says, *it is the man whom God accredits, not the man who takes credit to himself, that proves himself to be true metal;*[1] and if you're to live an interior life you must learn to enjoy his intimacy, unhampered by any interruption from the world outside.

Chapter 7

ON LOVING JESUS MORE THAN ANYTHING

It is a happy man that understands what is meant by loving Jesus and by despising oneself for his sake. You must renounce your other loves for the love of him, for Jesus desires to be loved alone more than all things else. When you love creatures, that love deceives you and never stays the same; when you love Jesus, your love is loyal and lasts. The man who clings to anything created will fall together with that fallible creature; if he holds fast to Jesus he will stay firm for ever. Give your love to him and keep him as your friend. When all others go away from you, he will not leave you or let you perish when the end comes. The day will come when, whether you like it or not, you must be parted from all men else.

2. In life and in death keep close to Jesus and give yourself into his faithful keeping; he alone can help you when all others fail you. He is of such a kind, this beloved friend of yours, that he will not share your love with another; he wishes to have your heart for himself alone, to reign there like a king seated on his rightful throne. If only you knew the way to empty your heart of all things created! If you did, how gladly would Jesus come and make his home with you! When you put your trust in men, excluding Jesus, you will find that it is nearly all a complete loss. Have no faith in a reed that shakes in the wind, don't try leaning upon it; *mortal things are but grass*, remember, *the glory of them is*

[1] 2 Cor. 10. 18.

but grass in flower[1] and will fall. Look only at a man's outward guise and you will quickly be led astray; look to others to console you and bring you benefit, and as often as not you will find you have suffered loss. If you look for Jesus in everything, you will certainly find him; but if it's yourself you're looking for, it's yourself you're going to find, and that to your own hurt, because a man is a greater bane to himself, if he doesn't look for Jesus, than the whole world is, or the whole host of his enemies.

Chapter 8

ON HAVING JESUS FOR A CLOSE FRIEND

When Jesus is beside us, all goes well and nothing seems hard; when he has gone, everything is difficult. When Jesus does not speak within us, human comfort is of little avail; when he speaks but a single word, we feel greatly comforted. Think of Mary Magdalen; how quickly she got up from the place she was weeping in, when Martha told her, *The Master is here and bids thee come.*[2] What a joyful hour it is, when Jesus calls us from our tears to bliss of soul! Without Jesus, how parched and hard of heart you are! How foolish and unwise of you, if you yearn for anything apart from Jesus! To lose Jesus is surely a greater loss than losing the whole world.

2. What can the world bestow upon you, if Jesus is not yours? Being without Jesus is hell's torment itself; being in his company is the very sweetness of paradise. With Jesus beside you, no enemy of yours will have power to do you harm. The man who finds Jesus finds a goodly treasure, a boon surpassing all others; the man who loses him loses a great deal indeed—he loses more than the whole world. The man who lives without Jesus is the poorest of the poor; and there is no one richer than the man who stands well with Jesus.

[1] Isaias 40. 6. [2] John 11. 28.

3. Knowing how to live one's life with Jesus is a great art; and knowing how to hold him fast is the peak of wisdom. Be humble, be a peacemaker, and Jesus will be with you; be devout and inwardly at rest, and he will remain with you. But should you have a mind to turn aside to outward things, you can quickly make Jesus flee from you, quickly lose his favour; and if you so send him away and lose him, whom will you have to flee to? What friend will you look for then? Without some friend, how is it possible for you to lead a good life? And if Jesus is not your friend above all others, you will be a very lonely and unhappy person. You would be a fool, then, if you placed your faith or your happiness in anyone else. You must prefer to have the whole world against you rather than slight Jesus. Of all who are dear to you, then, let Jesus alone be the object of your special affection.

4. We must love everybody for Jesus' sake, but Jesus for his own. Jesus Christ alone must be loved especially, seeing that he alone, above all others, is found to be a good and faithful friend. Because of him, and in him, let all men be dear to you, friends and foes alike; pray to him on behalf of them all, that they may come to know and love him. Never yearn for especial love or praise; that belongs to God alone, and he has no peer. Again, don't desire to have a monopoly of another's affections, or let that person have a monopoly of yours; just let Jesus be within you and every good soul.

5. Be pure and free at heart; don't let yourself get wrapped up in anything created. You must strip yourself bare and bring God a pure heart if you wish to be free to see how sweet the Lord is; and that you'll certainly never come to, unless you have his grace leading you on and guiding you. Only so, when you have cleared all else away, sent all else packing, may you become one with him, alone with him who is alone. It's like this; when the grace of God comes to a man, there's nothing he can't do. When it leaves him, he becomes poor and unsteady, abandoned, as it were, to the lash of misery. Now, when this happens, he oughtn't to give way to dejection and despair, but calmly stand ready to do

71

God's will and bear whatever befalls him, for the glory of Jesus Christ. Let him remember that summer follows winter, that day returns after night and that after a storm there comes a long spell of fine weather.

Chapter 9

ON LACKING ALL COMFORT

There's no great hardship in doing without human comfort, so long as we have the comfort of God behind us; what *is* difficult—immensely so—is the ability to do without both, God's comfort and man's, the will to endure cheerfully having one's heart an outcast from happiness, to seek in nothing one's own profit and to have no regard for one's own merit. What is there to boast about if you feel happy and devout when grace touches you? Times like that are what everyone longs for. The man who is carried by the grace of God rides pleasantly along; no wonder he feels no weariness, seeing he is carried by the Almighty and led by the chief Leader of all.

2. We gladly hold on to anything that brings us comfort; it goes against the grain for a man to strip himself of his attachment to self. Think how the holy martyr Laurence overcame the world, together with the priest he served; all that seemed delightful in the world he held in scorn; and for the love of Christ he even bore in patience the taking away from him of Sixtus, the high-priest of God, a man whom he loved most dearly. Thus by his love for his Creator he overcame his love for man, setting what pleased God before human comfort. So may you, too, learn to give up, for the love of God, those who are closest to you, the dearest of friends. You must not take it too much to heart when a friend deserts you; one day, you know, we must all be parted from one another at last.

3. It's a fierce struggle and a long one that a man must

wage in his heart before he learns complete self-mastery, learns to turn the whole of his affection towards God. When a man trusts in himself he easily falls into seeking human consolations; but when he truly loves Christ and diligently tries to be holy, there is no more falling back on such consolations, no seeking for the pleasures of the senses. What he looks for now is grievous toil and painful tasks to be endured for Christ's sake.

4. So, then, when God gives you spiritual comfort, take it and be thankful, mindful that it comes from God's bounty, not from any merit of yours. Don't let it make you proud, or overmuch happy, or full of foolish presumption; no, let the gift make you more humble, more careful in everything you do, more prudent in action. That state will pass away, to be succeeded by one of trial. When comfort is taken away from you, don't immediately give up hope; be humble and patient about it, and wait for the heavenly coming. God can give you back a consolation fuller than that you had before. To those who are well-versed in the ways of God, there is nothing new about this, nothing strange; the great Saints and the Prophets of old often suffered similar alternations of consolation and dryness of heart.

5. It was this that made someone say, when grace was with him: *I said in time of ease, Nothing can shake me now*; but when grace had left him, he tells us how he felt when he adds: *Then you turned your face away from me, and I was at peace no more.* Yet amid this distress he doesn't by any means despair, but begs the Lord all the more earnestly, saying: *I will cry to you, Lord, and call upon my God.* Finally, he has his prayer answered, and gives witness to that answer, when he says: *The Lord listened and had pity on me; the Lord became my helper.* In what way, though? *You have turned my mourning into joy*, he says; *and with gladness surrounded me.*[1] If that is the way God dealt with great Saints, we poor weaklings are not to give up hope if our hearts are sometimes afire and sometimes cold; that is because the spirit of God comes and goes according as it pleases his

[1] Ps. 29. 7-11.

will. It was this that made the holy Job say: *Never a day dawns but you will surprise him at his post; never a moment when you are not making proof of him.*[1]

6. What, then, am I to hope in, what am I to put my trust in, but in the great mercy of God alone, in nothing but the hope of heavenly grace? I may have at my side good men, devout brethren, loyal friends; I may have holy books or beautifully-written treatises, sweet-sounding chants and hymns; but it's little help they can give me, little spiritual zest, when grace has left me and I am alone with my poverty. At times like these there is no better remedy than patient self-abandonment to the will of God.

7. I have never come upon anyone, however religious and devout, who has not sometimes experienced a withdrawal of grace, felt a cooling-off of his fervour. Never a Saint has there been so rapt on high, so enlightened by God, that he has not, either before or after, been subject to temptation. That is because the man who has not been tested by some trouble or other for God's sake is unworthy to gaze on God's high mysteries. A temptation leading the way is frequently a sign that consolation will follow. It is to those who have been tried by temptation that heavenly consolation is promised. *Who wins the victory?* he says; *I will give him fruit from the tree of life.*[2]

8. God gives a man his consolation to make him stronger for bearing what goes against him; it is followed by temptation to prevent his becoming proud of his good deeds. The devil takes no sleep, and the flesh is not dead yet, so don't stop getting in trim for the fight; you have enemies to left and right of you, and they're always on the watch.

[1] Job 7. 18. [2] Apoc. 2. 7.

Chapter 10

ON BEING THANKFUL FOR GOD'S GRACE

Why look for rest, born as you are for toil? Better to look for things to suffer than for comfort, to be ready to carry your cross than to have a good time. What man in the world would not gladly welcome spiritual comfort and joy, if only he could keep it for good? For spiritual comfort surpasses all worldly delight, all pleasures of the flesh. All worldly pleasures are either empty or foul; those of the spirit alone are delightful and honourable, springing as they do from virtuous actions and being instilled by God into those who are pure of heart. There is no one, though, who is able to enjoy these heavenly consolations as he would like to, because the time of temptation is never long absent.

2. False freedom of heart and undue self-confidence are a great barrier to visitations from on high. God does well in making us a gift of his comfort and grace; but man does ill by not returning all to God, along with his gratitude. That is why the gifts of his grace cannot flow easily through us, because we are ungrateful to him from whom they come, not making a complete return of them to the spring from which they flow. A man who duly gives thanks for it will always have grace for the asking; what it is God's wont to give to the humble he will take from those who are proud.

3. I want no consolation that takes from me my sorrow for sin; I seek no contemplation that leads on to pride. High things, you know, are not necessarily holy things, nor sweet things good things; not every desire is a pure one, nor are all the things we hold dear pleasing to God. If a grace makes me more humble, more prudent, more ready to renounce my own desires, then I bid it welcome with all my heart. When a man has been taught by receiving the gift of grace and chastened by bearing the lash of its withdrawal, he won't dare to attribute any good to himself; no, he will readily acknowledge his poverty and nakedness. Give God his proper due, and enter what is yours on your own

account. Be grateful, I mean, to God for his grace, and realize that guilt and the punishment due to it belong to you alone.

4. Always put yourself in the lowest place, and you will be given the highest; because the highest cannot stand without the lowest. Those Saints stand highest in God's sight who are lowest in their own; the more glory is theirs, the more humble they are at heart. Full as they are of truth and heavenly glory, they do not hanker after glory that means nothing; with God for their strength and support, they are quite incapable of giving themselves airs. Those who attribute entirely to God whatever good they have received do not seek glory from one another; the glory they seek for is that which comes from God alone. What they long for above all else is that God should be praised both in themselves and in all the Saints; that is the end to which all their actions are constantly directed.

5. When you are given a little, then, be thankful for it, and you will deserve to receive more. Reckon a small gift as a great one, a slight favour as a special award. When you consider who it is who gives these things, no gift of his will seem small or petty; no present is small that comes from God on high. Even though his gift should be one of punishment and affliction, we should welcome it all the same, because whatever he allows to happen to us he brings about in the interests of our salvation. If you long to keep the grace of God, be thankful for grace when it is given to you, patient when it is withdrawn. Pray for it to return, and be humbly watchful, so as not to miss it when it comes.

Chapter 11

ON THE FEWNESS OF THOSE
WHO LOVE THE CROSS OF JESUS

Jesus today has many who love his heavenly kingdom, but few who carry his cross; many who yearn for comfort, few who long for distress. Plenty of people he finds to share his banquet, few to share his fast. Everyone desires to take part in his rejoicing, but few are willing to suffer anything for his sake. There are many that follow Jesus as far as the breaking of bread, few as far as drinking the cup of suffering; many that revere his miracles, few that follow him in the indignity of his cross; many that love Jesus as long as nothing runs counter to them; many that praise and bless him, as long as they receive some comfort from him; but should Jesus hide from them and leave them for a while, they fall to complaining or become deeply depressed.

2. Those who love Jesus for his own sake, not for the sake of their own comfort, bless him in time of trouble and heartache as much as when they are full of consolation; and should it never be his will to grant them any comfort, they would still always praise him, always long to thank him.

3. To love Jesus purely, with no alloy of self-interest and self-love, is a source of great power. Mercenaries—isn't that the proper name for those who are always looking for comfort? Those who are always thinking of their own profit and advantage are shewn up as lovers of themselves rather than of Christ. Where will you find a man willing to serve God without hope of reward?

4. Rarely will you find anyone so spiritual as to be stripped bare of all things. Who will shew me a man truly poor in spirit, completely severed from all things created? Such a one is *a rare treasure, brought from distant shores.*[1] If a man were to give away everything he had, it would still be nothing; if he did severe penance, it would still be but little; if he were to have a grasp of all knowledge, he would still be a long way off. Even if he had great holiness and fervent devotion, there would still be much lacking to him; that one thing, I mean, which he needs above all else. And what is this one thing? That, having left all things behind, he should leave himself, renounce himself completely, keeping back nothing of his self-love; and when he has done everything that he knows he ought to do, let him realize that he has done nothing.

[1] Prov. 31.10.

5. It is not for him to reckon as a great achievement what might seem so in other men's eyes; no, he should admit the truth, admit that he is a worthless servant. It is Truth himself who tells us: *When you have done all that was commanded you, you are to say, We are servants, and worthless.*[1] Then indeed will he be able to be naked and poor in spirit, saying along with the prophet: *You see me friendless and forlorn.*[2] For all that, there is never a man richer, none with greater power, greater freedom, than he who knows how to renounce himself and all besides, setting himself in the lowest place of all.

Chapter 12

ON THE ROYAL ROAD OF THE HOLY CROSS

"Renounce yourself, take up your cross and follow Jesus." There are many to whom that seems a hard saying; but how much harder will it be to hear that word of final judgement: *Go far from me, you that are accursed, into eternal fire.*[3] Those who now gladly hear the word of the cross and keep what it commands will not be afraid then when they hear the doom of everlasting loss. It is this sign of the cross that will appear in the sky when the Lord comes to judge us. Then all the servants of the cross, who during their lifetime made the Crucified the pattern of their deeds, will come with great confidence before Christ who is to judge them.

2. Why, then, are you afraid to take up your cross? It is your road to the kingdom of Christ. In the cross lies our salvation, our life; in the cross we have a defence against our foes. In the cross we have a pouring-in of heavenly sweetness, a strengthening of our minds and spiritual joy. In the cross is the peak of virtue, the perfection of holiness. There is no salvation for our souls, no hope of life everlasting, but in the cross. Take up your cross,

[1] Luke 17. 10.   [2] Ps. 24. 16.   [3] Matt. 25. 41.

then, and follow Jesus; and you will go into life that has no end. He has gone ahead of you, bearing his own cross; on that cross he has died for you, that you may bear your own cross and on that cross yearn to die. If you have died together with him, together with him you will have life; if you have shared his suffering you will also share his glory.

3. You see, the cross is at the root of everything; everything is based upon our dying there. There is no other road to life, to true inward peace, but the road of the cross, of dying daily to self. Walk where you will, seek whatever you have a mind to; you will find no higher road above, no safer road below, than the road of the holy cross. You may make all your plans and arrangements in accordance with your own notions and desires; even so, you will always find you have some suffering to bear, whether you like it or not; you will always find the cross.

Either you will be conscious of bodily pain, or your soul will be inwardly in distress.

4. Sometimes God will leave you to yourself, sometimes your neighbour will get on your nerves; what is worse, you will often become burdensome to your own self. No remedy or comfort will have power to free you from this condition, to make it easier to bear; you must put up with it as long as God so wills. God wants you to learn to bear suffering without anything to comfort you, to surrender yourself completely to him, to gain in humility by passing through distress. There is no one who so deeply realizes what Christ went through as the man who has had to suffer as he did. The cross, then, is at all times ready for you; never a place on earth but you will find it awaiting you. Dash off here or there, you can't get away from it; because, wherever you go, you take yourself along with you, and at every moment you will find yourself. Look above yourself or below, outside yourself or within; everywhere you will find the cross. And everywhere you must keep patient, if you would have inward peace and gain an everlasting crown.

5. If you carry your cross willingly, it will carry you and

bring you to the goal for which you long. There, as you know, suffering will come to an end; but that won't be while you are still here. If you grudge carrying your cross, it becomes a burden that weighs you down all the more; yet carry it you must. If you reject one cross, you will certainly find another; and this time it may not be so light.

6. Do you think you can escape something that never mortal man has been able to avoid? Think of the Saints; which of them spent his time in this world without the cross, without suffering? Why, even our Lord, Jesus Christ, was never for a single hour free from pain and suffering the whole of his lifetime. *Was it not to be expected*, he said, *that the Christ should undergo these sufferings, and enter so into his glory?*[1] Then how can you look for any other road than this royal road, the road of the holy cross?

7. The whole life of Christ was a cross and a martyrdom; and you go looking for rest and mirth! If you look for anything else but suffering to bear, you are right off the road; because the whole of this mortal life is full of misery, marked with crosses in every direction. The higher a man rises in the ways of the spirit, the weightier will he often find his crosses becoming. That is because the more his love of God grows, the more painful he feels this state of exile from him.

8. Such a man, however, afflicted as he is in so many ways, does not lack consolation to relieve him, because he realizes how great profit he is acquiring by bearing his cross. For while he willingly surrenders himself to it, his whole burden of suffering is changed into confident hope that God will console him. The more the flesh is weakened by suffering, the more is the spirit strengthened by means of inward grace. It not seldom happens that a man is so strengthened by his desire for suffering and adversity, the effect of his love that would follow the pattern of the cross of Christ, that he has no wish ever to be free from pain and suffering. This is because of his belief that the more affliction he has been able to bear for God's sake, the heavier to endure, the more pleasing he will be in God's sight. All this does not come from a man's

[1] Luke 24. 26.

own strength, but from the grace of Christ, which can have so powerful an effect, working as it does in our weak human nature; so that what a man of his nature shrinks from and seeks to escape he will go to meet and choose to love, through the fire of the spirit that burns within him.

9. Man by himself is not given to bearing crosses or loving them; to chastening his body and making it his slave; to avoiding honours and willingly brooking insults; to thinking little of himself and hoping that others will do the same. It is not his way to put up with all kinds of opposition and loss and not to desire any prosperity in this world. If you look only to yourself, all this kind of thing will be beyond your power; but if you put your trust in the Lord, you will be given strength from heaven, enabled to lord it over the world and the flesh. Even your enemy, the Devil, will be powerless to make you afraid, if you wear the armour of faith and are signed with the cross of Christ.

10. Set out, then, as a good and faithful servant of Christ, to bear like a man the cross of your Lord, that cross to which he was nailed for love of you. Be prepared to endure much thwarting and many a difficulty in this life of sadness; because that's how things are going to be for you, wherever you are, that's how you're sure to find things, wherever you look for shelter from them. That's the way it's got to be; there's no cure, no getting round the fact of trouble and sorrow; you just have to put up with them. If you long to be the Lord's friend, to share what is his, you must drink his cup and like it. As for consolations, let God see about that; he will arrange about that kind of thing as he sees best. Your job must be to be ready to endure troubles and to reckon them the greatest of comforts; for what we suffer in this present life is nothing when we compare it with the glory to be won in the life to come, even though you alone were able to endure it all.

11. When you have reached such a point that trouble is sweet to you, something to be relished for Christ's sake, you may reckon that all is well with you; you have found heaven on earth. But so long as suffering irks you, so long as you

try to avoid it, things will go ill with you; everywhere you will be pursued by the pain you try to escape.

12. If you resolve, as you ought, to suffer and to die, things will at once go better with you and you will find peace. Even if, like St Paul, you were to be caught up to the third heaven, that would be no guarantee of your suffering no further affliction. *I have yet to tell him,* says Jesus, *how much suffering he will have to undergo for my name's sake.*[1] You have still to suffer, then, if you wish to love Jesus and serve him for ever.

13. If only you were worthy to suffer in some way for the name of Jesus! What great glory you would have awaiting you! How all the Saints of God would rejoice! And think how you would strengthen the spiritual life of your neighbour! All men agree in applauding patience in suffering; few are willing to suffer. You ought gladly to suffer a little for Christ's sake; there are many who suffer far worse for worldly interests.

14. Make no mistake about it; the life you are to lead must be one of death-in-life. The more a man dies to himself, the more he begins to live to God. No one is fit to grasp heavenly things unless he resigns himself to bearing affliction for Christ's sake. There is nothing more acceptable to God, nothing so conducive to your soul's health in this world, than willingly to suffer for Christ's sake. If you had the choice, you ought to choose rather to suffer affliction for Christ's sake than to be refreshed by much comfort; that would make you resemble Christ more nearly, make you follow more closely the pattern of all the Saints. Our merit, you see, our progress in virtue, doesn't consist of enjoying much heavenly sweetness and consolation; no, it lies in bearing heavy affliction and trouble.

15. If there had been anything better for men, more profitable for their salvation, than suffering, you may be sure that Christ, by his teaching and by his own example, would have pointed it out. But no; addressing the disciples who were following him, and all those who wish to follow

[1] Acts 9. 16.

him, he clearly urges them to carry the cross, when he says: *If any man has a mind to come my way, let him renounce self, and take up his cross, and follow me.*[1] So then, when we have made an end of reading and studying, this is the conclusion we should reach at last: *that we cannot enter the kingdom of heaven without many trials.*[2]

[1] Luke 9. 23.   [2] Acts 14. 21.

BOOK III

ON INWARD CONSOLATION

Chapter 1

ON THE WAY CHRIST
SPEAKS INWARDLY TO THE SOUL

Let me listen, now, to the voice of the Lord God.[1] Blessed is
the soul that hears the Lord speaking within her and receives
from his lips words that bring her comfort. Blessed are the
ears that catch the soft whisper of God's voice and pay no
heed to the muttering voices of this world; blessed indeed
the ears that listen not to the voices that ring out around
them, but to him who inwardly teaches the truth. Blessed
are the eyes that are shut to things outside, their gaze fixed
on inward things. Blessed are those who make their way
through to the heart of the inward life, who strive daily
more and more to prepare themselves for the reception of
heavenly secrets. Blessed are those who long to give all their
time to God and shake themselves free of all the trammels
of this world. My soul, here is something for you to heed;
shut fast the doors in the face of all that comes through the
senses, that so you may hear what the Lord your God is
speaking within you.

2. This is what your Beloved says: "I am your well-being,
your peace, your life. Keep close beside me, and you will
find peace. Let go of all things that pass away and seek
those that last for ever. What are all the things of time but
things that lead you away from me? What help is there for
you in anything created if he who made you forsakes you?
Then give up your claim to all else and make yourself a
faithful and pleasing servant of your Creator; so will you
be enabled to bring real happiness within your grasp."

[1] Ps. 84. 9.

Chapter 2

TRUTH SPEAKS WITHIN US
WITHOUT THE OUTWARD SOUND OF WORDS

The Learner: Speak on, Lord; your servant is listening.[1]
Perfect in your own servant's heart the knowledge of your will.[2]
Incline my heart to the words of your mouth; here are warnings that must soak in like the dew.[3] In the days of old the
people of Israel said to Moses: *Do you tell us the message;
we are ready to obey you. Do not let us hear the Lord speaking; it will cost us our lives.*[4] No, Lord, that is not the way I
pray; instead, I join with the prophet Samuel in beseeching
you thus: *Speak on, Lord; your servant is listening.* It is not
Moses or any of the prophets that I want to speak to me;
it is you, Lord, whose voice I want to hear, you from whom
the prophets draw their inspiration and enlightenment. No
need to use them; you by yourself can fully instruct me,
whereas they without you would be quite unavailing.

2. The words of the prophets may ring out, but they cannot bring me your spirit. They speak in beautiful language;
but, should you keep silence, they fail to set the heart afire.
They express but the letter of your message; it is for you to
lay bare the meaning within. They bring mysteries to our
notice; you unfold the meaning of what they speak but in
signs. They tell us what your commandments are; you help
us to keep them. They point out the way; you give us
strength to walk upon it. They affect us only from outside;
you teach and enlighten the very heart. They water from
without the seed of your word; it is you who make it bear
fruit. They cry aloud in words; it is you who make us
understand what we hear.

3. Then let not Moses speak to me, but you, my Lord and
my God, you the eternal Truth; otherwise I may die and
bear no fruit, if I have been warmed only from outside and
not been kindled to flame within. When the judgement
comes, do not let me be ranked with those who heard the

[1] 1 Kings 3. 9. [2] Ps. 77. 1. [3] Deut. 32. 2. [4] Exod. 20. 19.

word and failed to obey it, knew it and did not love it, believed it and failed to keep it. *Speak on, then, Lord; your servant is listening; your words are the words of eternal life.*[1] Speak to me; let your words comfort me in whatever way you will, and help me to amend my whole life; and may they bring you praise and glory and honour without end.

Chapter 3

WE SHOULD LISTEN HUMBLY TO GOD'S WORDS; MANY PEOPLE FAIL TO APPRECIATE THEM PROPERLY

The Beloved: My son, listen to my words; words of surpassing sweetness they are, words that outsoar all the learning of the philosophers and wise men of this world. My words are spirit and life; they have no place in the scales of man's understanding. They should not be brought out to satisfy the unthinking pleasure they afford you; no, they should be listened to in silence, received with humility and deep affection.

2. I said this once, too: *Happy, Lord, is the man whom you chasten, reading him the lesson of your law! For him, you will lighten the time of adversity;*[2] he will not be left lonely upon the earth.

3. From the very beginning—it is I, the Lord, speaking —I taught the prophets, and from then until the present day I have never stopped speaking to all men; but many there are who are deaf to my voice and hard of heart. Many are fonder of listening to the world than to God, readier to follow the cravings of the flesh than what God wants of them. The world promises men its petty prizes that are soon gone, and finds in them its eager and willing slaves; I promise them prizes whose glory lasts for ever, and the hearts of men are dull and unmoved. What man is there who in all he does gives me such devotion, such obedience,

[1] John 6. 68. [2] Ps. 93. 12.

as is given the world and those who rule the world? *Sidon, blush for shame, says the sea.*[1] If you ask why this should be so, I will tell you the reason. To gain some trifling reward, a man will hurry a long way; yet there are many who, to gain eternal life, will hardly take one single step. People aim at prizes of little worth; sometimes you hear of sordid wrangling over a single coin; for some minor advantage, or the bare promise of it, they will wear themselves out, toiling day and night.

4. And yet—shame on them!—when they are offered a good that cannot change, a reward beyond price, honour and glory without end, how loth they are to bear even the least amount of toil! Well may you blush, you slothful and complaining servant, that men such as these are readier to lose their souls than you are to win life. They get more enjoyment from their chasing after vanities than you do in the pursuit of truth. The hopes they cherish are often belied; no one is deceived by my promises. The man who trusts in me is never sent away empty. When I promise a thing, I give it; when I speak, I make good my word, if only a man remains faithful in my love to the end. I am he who rewards all good men, strong in my praise of all who are devout.

5. Write these words of mine in your heart and carefully think them over; when the time comes for you to be tempted, you will find them a great standby. There will be things in your reading you fail to understand; their meaning will come home to you at the time of my coming. There are two ways in which I visit my chosen, one by testing their loyalty, the other by bringing them comfort. There are likewise two lessons that I read them every day; in one I rebuke them for their misdeeds, in the other I encourage them to grow in virtue. *The man who makes me of no account, and does not accept my words, has a judge appointed to try him; it is the message I have uttered that will be his judge at the last day.*[2]

[1] Isaias 23. 4.　[2] John 12. 48.

A PRAYER BEGGING FOR THE GRACE OF DEVOTION

6. O Lord my God, you are my total good; who am I, to dare speak to you? I am the least, the poorest of your servants, nothing but a wretched little worm, far poorer and more insignificant than I know or have the courage to say. Yet remember, Lord, that I am nothing, possess nothing, can do nothing. You alone are good, just and holy. You can do all things, grant all things, fill all things, leaving none but the sinner empty of your bounty. Remember your mercies; fill my heart with your grace, for it is not your wish that any of your works should be empty.

7. How can I bear this my life of sorrow, if you do not support me with your mercy and grace? Do not turn your face away from me; do not be long in coming to me; do not withdraw your consolation from me, or my soul will become like a land parched with drought. Lord, teach me to do what you want me to do. Teach me to live humbly and worthily in your presence. You are my wisdom; you know me as I really am, as you have done before the world was made, before by birth I came into this world.

Chapter 4

WE SHOULD LIVE HUMBLY AND
WITHOUT PRETENCE IN THE SIGHT OF GOD

The Beloved: My son, walk without pretence in my sight, ever seeking me in singleness of heart. The man who so walks in my sight will be shielded from the assaults of evil; the truth will free him from those who would lead him astray and from the backbiting of the wicked. If it is the truth that frees you, you will be free indeed; the vain words of men will leave you unconcerned

The Learner: Lord, what you say is true; so let it be with me, I beg you. Let the truth be my teacher, my guard, and my preserver until at last I reach salvation. Let it free me from every evil affection, every ill-regulated love, and I will walk beside you in utter freedom of heart.

2. *The Beloved:* I will teach you (says Truth) what is right and pleasing in my sight. With great grief and regret recall your sins to mind; never imagine yourself to be of any account because of the good deeds you may have done. The plain fact is this: you are a sinner, the prey of the many passions with which you are enmeshed. Left to yourself, you can never get anywhere; you soon fall away, soon lose the battle, are soon confused, soon unmanned. You have nothing to brag about, much that should make you take a poor view of yourself; you are much weaker than you think.

3. Nothing, then, of all you do should seem to you a great achievement. Indeed, you should think nothing great, nothing precious or remarkable, nothing worth your consideration, but what is eternal; nor should you think anything sublime or a fit object of your praise and your desire, but what is eternal. More than all else, it is the eternal truth that should be your delight; your grief should always spring from the consciousness of your own utter wretchedness. There is nothing you should fear more than your own sins and vices, nothing you should think worthier of blame, nothing you should take more care to avoid; they ought to be a greater source of grief to you than the loss of anything you possess. There are some people who lack sincerity in their actions when in my presence. These, in their curiosity and conceit, would know my secrets and understand the sublime mysteries of God, neglecting themselves and their salvation. Such men, when I bar their way, often fall into great temptations and sins, the fault of their own pride and curiosity.

4. Dread the judgements of God; be afraid of the anger of him who is almighty. Do not search into the actions of the Most High; rather let your searching be for your own sins —how often and how grievously you have offended, the number of good deeds you have failed to do. Some people carry their devotion only in books, others in pictures, others again in outward signs and representations. There are

some who have me on their lips, but not much in their heart. There are those, too, whose understanding has been enlightened, whose affections have been purified; they sigh with longing for eternal life. Hearing of worldly matters depresses them, they satisfy but reluctantly the needs of bodily existence. Men such as these are well aware what it is that the spirit of truth speaks within them. This is the lesson he gives them: to look down on the things of earth and to love the things of heaven; to disregard the world, and, day-long, night-long, to thirst for heaven.

Chapter 5

ON THE WONDERFUL EFFECT OF DIVINE LOVE

The Learner: Father in heaven, Father of Jesus Christ my Lord, I bless you for deigning to remember me and my poverty. Father of mercies, God of all comfort, I thank you for refreshing me with your comfort, little though I deserve any comfort at all. To you and your only-begotten Son, together with the Holy Ghost, the Comforter, I give blessing and glory always, both now and for ages without end. Ah, Lord God, you the holy one, you my lover, when you come into my heart, the whole of my inmost being will leap with joy. You are my glory, the comfort of my heart; my stronghold and my refuge in my hour of peril.

2. As yet I am but weak in love, unsure in virtue; that is why I need your support, your comfort. So come to me, come to me often and teach me what is in your holy laws. Set me free from evil passions; heal my heart of all its ill-regulated affections; so that, whole and pure in my inmost being, I may become ready to love, strong to endure suffering, steadfast to persevere.

3. A mighty force it is, this thing love, mighty and altogether good; alone it takes the weight from every burden, alone it bears evenly the uneven load. It bears a burden as

if no burden were there, makes the bitter things of life sweet and good to taste. To love Jesus is a wondrous thing; it urges men on to mighty deeds, stirs up in them the desire for a life ever more holy. Love must be ever mounting on high, unfettered by things below; love would ever be free, a stranger to every worldly desire, fearful lest its inward vision grow clouded, lest some worldly gain should encumber its advance, some worldly misfortune bring it headlong down. There is nothing sweeter than love, nothing stronger, nothing higher, nothing wider, nothing fuller, nothing better in heaven or earth; for love is born of God, and only in God, above all that he has created, can it find rest.

4. A man in love treads on air; he runs for very joy. He is a free man; nothing can hold him back. He gives all for all, finding his rest in one who is high above all else, the source and origin of all that is good. For gifts he has no regard, but turns to him who is their giver, who is above all good gifts. Love often knows no limits; its impetuous fire leaps across every boundary. Love feels no burden, makes light of toil, strives for things beyond its strength. Love never tries to make out that anything is impossible; everything, in the eyes of love, is both possible and lawful. Love, then, can do everything; many a task there is that love can fulfil and many a wish it can make effective, where the man who does not love is powerless and fails.

5. Love is ever on the watch; it rests, but does not slumber, is wearied but not spent, alarmed but not dismayed; like a living flame, a blazing torch, it shoots upward, fearlessly passing through aught that bars its path. If anyone has this love, he will know what I mean. A loud cry in the ears of God is that burning love for him in the soul which says: "My God, my love, you are all mine and I all yours."

6. Let my love know no bounds; let me learn to taste with the lips of my inmost being how sweet it is to love, to melt in love's fire, to float on the waves of love! Let love keep hold of me, as in unwonted fervour and wonder I rise above

my usual self. Let me sing the song of love and follow you, my Beloved, to high heaven; let my soul grow faint in praising you, rejoicing in your love. Let me love you more than myself, love myself only for your sake; let me love in you all who truly love you—that is the bidding of the law of love, that law whose light streams forth from you.

7. Love is swift, pure, dutiful, pleasant and agreeable; it is strong, patient, faithful, prudent, long-suffering, manly, never seeking its own advantage. For when anyone seeks that, he falls away from love. Love is wary, humble and upright; it is not soft, not unstable, not intent on empty trifles; it is sober, chaste, steadfast, keeping due watch on all the senses. Love is submissive and obedient to those in authority, mean and contemptible in its own regard. To God it is ever devout and thankful, ever trusting and hoping in him even when it cannot taste his sweetness; for there is no living a life of love without sorrow.

8. The man who is not ready to endure everything and stand fast by the will of his Beloved does not deserve to be called a lover; a lover should be glad to welcome all sorts of hardship and bitterness for the sake of his Beloved, and never let himself turn away from him when things go against him.

Chapter 6

ON THE TESTING OF A TRUE LOVER

The Beloved: My son, you are not yet a strong and experienced lover.—How is that, Lord?—Because the moment you come to the slightest obstacle you give up what you have begun and seek for comfort with the utmost eagerness. The brave lover stands fast in temptation, gives no credit to the subtle suggestions of his enemy the Devil. When things go well with him, I am his delight; so am I still when he meets with trouble.

2. An experienced lover heeds not so much the gift of

the lover as the love of him that gave it. What he looks for is affection, not money; his Beloved is higher in his eyes than any gift. A noble lover does not rest content with a gift; he desires me rather·than any gift I can make him. All is not lost, therefore, if you sometimes feel less love for me or my Saints than you would like to. That good, sweet feeling you are aware of now and then is brought about by my grace working in you at that time; a kind of foretaste of your heavenly home. You must not depend too much upon it, though; it is a thing that comes and goes. What *is* a sure sign of virtue and of great merit is to fight against evil stirrings of the mind when they arise and to treat with contempt the suggestions of the Devil.

3. You must not be disturbed, then, by fancies foreign to your real self, whatever it may be that causes them. Keep bravely to your resolutions, hold on to your good intent towards God. It is no illusion if sometimes you are suddenly caught up in ecstasy and immediately return to the usual frivolous thoughts that crowd your heart. Such thoughts you put up with rather than encourage, and so long as you find them distasteful and struggle against them, you may count them as gain and not as loss.

4. You know, the Devil, that old enemy of yours, tries by every means he can to obstruct your desire to do good, and to lure you away from any kind of devout exercise; honouring the Saints, for example, devout meditation upon my sufferings, profitable recalling of your sins, keeping watch over your heart, and your firm resolve to advance in holiness. Many are the evil thoughts he slips into your mind, to fill you with weariness and disgust, hoping so to entice you from prayer and reading good books.

A humble confession is abhorrent to him, and he would make you give up Communion if he could. Do not believe him; pay no attention to him, however often he spreads out his crafty nets to catch you. When he suggests evil and filthy thoughts, tell him they are his, not yours. Speak to him like this: "You filthy spirit, be off with you! Blush, you wretch! How utterly filthy you are, putting stuff like that in my ears! Away from me, you traitor, you monster of evil, you shall have no hold upon me. Jesus will be beside me, like a valiant warrior, and you will stand there confounded. I would rather die, rather undergo any kind of torment, than give in to you. So keep quiet and hold your tongue; I'm not going to listen to you any more, however often you try annoying me." *The Lord is my light and my deliverance; whom have I to fear?*[1] *Though a whole host were arrayed against me, my heart would be undaunted.*[2] *God is our refuge and stronghold.*[3]

5. Fight on like a good soldier; if you fall now and then through weakness, pluck up greater courage than before, trusting that my grace, too, will be more abundant. Be particularly on the watch against foolish self-satisfaction and conceit; that is a thing that leads many people into error, sometimes making them fall into almost incurable blindness of heart. Take warning by their downfall; let the thought of these conceited fools who presumed in their own powers keep you always humble.

Chapter 7

ON CONCEALING GRACE
AND MAKING HUMILITY ITS GUARDIAN

The Beloved: My son, it is more to your advantage, more to your safety, if you conceal the grace of devotion; you must not boast of it, must not talk much about it, must not set too high a value on it. Instead, you should think the worse of yourself and fear that grace has been given to one who does not deserve it. You are not to cling too tightly to such feelings of devotion; they can soon change into just the opposite. When you are aware of such grace, think how wretched and helpless you always are without it. When you receive the grace of divine comfort, it is not a sign of much progress in the spiritual life; you *are* making progress,

[1] Ps. 26. 1.   [2] Ps. 26. 3.   [3] Ps. 39. 18.

though, if you bear the withdrawal of grace with patience, humility and resignation, not flagging in your zeal for prayer nor completely abandoning the other acts of devotion you are in the habit of performing. Do willingly whatever you can, as best you can and as seems best to you; do not give up attending to your soul on account of any dryness or mental torment you may feel.

2. There are many people who, as soon as things go contrary to them, immediately become impatient or lose heart. The road a man is to tread is not always his to decide; it is for God to give and to comfort, when he wills, in the measure he wills and whom he wills, as seems good to him and no more. Some people, for want of prudence, have brought about their own downfall through the grace of devotion. They wanted to do more than they were able, taking no account of their own littleness, but obeying the urges of their heart rather than what reason judged to be right. Because they presumed to greater things than God wanted them to, they soon lost his grace. They had built themselves a nest in heaven, and they found themselves forsaken, in want and wretchedness; they were thus brought low, thus deprived of their wealth, to teach them not to fly with their own wings but to nestle beneath the refuge of my own. Those who are still new and unaccustomed to the way of the Lord can easily make mistakes, easily go astray, unless they have the advice of wise men to guide them.

3. If they mean to follow their own ideas rather than trust others of known experience, their end will be imperilled, but only if they refuse to be weaned from their own conceit. People who think themselves wise are rarely humble enough to let others guide them. It is better to know but little, to be not very clever, and to be humble about it, than to own vast stocks of knowledge, if you are so foolish as to be self-important about it. You are better off with a little, if having a lot is going to make you conceited. A man is far from being wise when he gives himself up wholly to joy, forgetting his former poverty and that pure dread of the Lord which is fearful of losing the grace which has

been offered to it. A man is likewise far from being virtuous who in time of trouble and difficulty abandons all hope and harbours thoughts and feelings about me which lack that trust he ought to have.

4. You will often find that a man who in peacetime hasn't a worry in the world becomes extremely depressed when war comes and a prey to many fears. If you knew how to remain always humble and unimportant in your own eyes, knew how to give your spirit proper guidance and direction, you would not fall so quickly into danger and wrongdoing. When the flame of devotion has been kindled in your heart, it is a good idea to consider what is going to happen when that light fails. At such a time, remember that the light may return once more, that I have withdrawn it from you for a time to give you warning and to give glory to myself.

6. When I test you like that, it is often more to your advantage than if things always went the way you wanted them to. A man is not to be accounted as full of merit for often seeing visions or feeling divine consolation, or being a great Biblical scholar or being raised to a higher dignity. No, a man is meritorious when his spiritual life is based on real humility, when he is full of the love of God; when he is always seeking, purely and wholly, the honour of God; when he thinks of himself as good for nothing, really takes a poor view of himself, and is much happier when others look down on him and humiliate him than when they honour him.

Chapter 8

ON TAKING A HUMBLE VIEW OF ONESELF IN GOD'S SIGHT

The Learner: Dust and ashes though I be, I have taken it upon me to speak to my Lord.[1] If I think anything more of myself than that, you stand on the opposite side of the
[1] Gen. 18. 27.

court, while my sins give evidence, true evidence I cannot deny. But if I admit my insignificance, confess I am but nothing, turn away from all my self-importance and bring myself down to the level of the dust that I am, your grace will be merciful towards me, your light will be close to my heart; and all my self-esteem, infinitesimal though it be, will be drowned in the abyss of my own nothingness and be for ever no more. That is the way you shew me my real self—what I am, what I have been, what I have become; because I am nothing, and did not even know it. Left to myself, I am but nothing, a mere mass of weakness; the moment you look upon me, I at once become strong and filled with fresh joy. Your raising me so speedily, embracing me so tenderly, overwhelms me with amazement, seeing that the weight of my own sinfulness is always dragging me downward.

2. It is your love that brings this about, freely forestalling me and coming to my help in my countless needs, guarding me from grave dangers and snatching me away, as I am bound to confess, from evils past reckoning. It was through loving myself in the wrong way that I lost myself; by seeking you alone and loving you sincerely, I have found both myself and you. My love for you has made me shrivel even more completely into the nothingness that I am. You deal with me, my dearest love, far above what I deserve, far above anything I dare hope for or ask for.

3. My God, may you be blessed; for though I am unworthy of any kindness, yet your generosity, your limitless bounty, never ceases to do good even to those who are ungrateful, to those who have turned far away from you. Turn us back to you, that we may be grateful, humble and devout; for you are our souls' health, our virtue, our strength.

Chapter 9

EVERYTHING IS TO BE SEEN
IN ITS RELATION TO GOD, OUR LAST END

The Beloved: If you really want to be happy, my son, you must make me your supreme and final end. Too frequently your affections stoop down to embrace yourself and things created; direct them on me, and they will be cleansed. When you seek yourself in anything, you at once lose heart and grow dry within. You ought therefore to refer everything chiefly to me; after all, it is I who have given you everything. Look upon each particular thing as flowing forth from the supreme good; that is the reason why it is to me, as to their origin, that all things must be brought back.

2. From me, as from a living spring, all men draw the water of life, little and great alike, rich and poor. Those who serve me freely and willingly shall receive grace for grace; but the man who would glory in anything apart from me, delight in some good of his own, will have no firm foothold in real joy. His heart will not be opened wide within him, but in a multitude of ways he will be thwarted and hemmed in. So, then, don't go writing good deeds down on your own account and don't attribute goodness to any man; give it all to God, without whom man has nothing. I have given you all, and I want to have it all back; what I ask of you, and that with great insistence, is that you should be thankful.

3. There you have the truth, the truth that sends vain-glory about its business. If heavenly grace gains entrance to your heart, together with real charity, there will be no envy there, no shrivelling of the heart, no monopolizing of your affections by any particular love. The divine charity overcomes everything, gives every power of the soul room to expand. If you are really wise, you will place all your joy, all your hope, in no one but me, because *none is good except God only*,[1] and he is above all things to be praised, and in all things blessed.

[1] Luke 18. 19.

Chapter 10

ON THE JOY OF SERVING GOD
AND SCORNING THE WORLD

The Learner: Lord, I cannot keep silent; I will now speak
yet again, utter my mind in the ears of my God, my Lord,
my King, who dwells on high. *What treasures of loving-
kindness, Lord, do you store up for the men who fear you!*[1]
But what are you to those who love you, to those who
serve you with all their heart? There are no words to des-
cribe the sweetness of that sight of yourself which you
lavish on those who love you. No greater proof have you
shewn me of the tenderness of your love for me than this:
that when I had no being, you brought me into existence;
and that when I went straying afar from you, you brought
me back to your service and taught me to love you.

2. O spring of unfailing love, what am I to say about you?
How can I forget you, you who did not disdain to remember
me, even when I was rotten with sin and lost to grace? You
have shewn mercy to your servant beyond anything he
could have hoped for; beyond anything he deserved, you
have given him your grace and your friendship. How can I
pay you back for grace such as that? It is not given to
everyone to forsake all things, abjure the world and take
up the monastic life. Is there anything so very wonderful
in my serving you? After all, the whole of creation is bound
to do that. No, I ought not to think I am doing anything
wonderful in serving you; what really does astound me is
that, for all your greatness, you are willing to have as your
servant a poor good-for-nothing like me, willing to rank
him with your best-beloved servants.

3. You know, Lord, everything I have is yours, even the
very tools of my service. But really it's the other way about;
you serve me rather than I you. Heaven and earth, which
you made for the use of man, stand ready to be of service,
fulfilling day in, day out, whatever commands you give

[1] Ps. 30. 20.

them. And that's nothing; why, you have appointed the very Angels to serve the needs of man. But all this is far surpassed by your stooping to serve man yourself, your promise to give yourself to him.

4. What shall I give you in return for all these innumerable kindnesses? Oh, if only I could serve you all the days of my life; if only I were good enough to serve you worthily even for a single day! You are indeed worthy of all service, all honour, and praise without end. You are indeed my Lord, and I your poor servant, bound to serve you with all my might; I should never grow weary of praising you. That is what I want to do, that is my desire; whatever in me is wanting, I count on your kindness to make good.

5. A great honour it is, a thing to make one really proud, to be in your service and for your sake to despise everything else. Great will be the grace bestowed on those who have volunteered to be in your most holy service. Men who for love of you have renounced all the pleasures of the flesh will find instead the comfort of the Holy Ghost in all its sweetness. Those who for the sake of your name enter the narrow way and have nothing to do with worldly employments will be rewarded with great spiritual freedom.

6. How joyful and pleasant a thing it is to serve God! It is by serving him that man becomes truly free and holy. How blessed is the lot of those who serve God in the religious life! Such a life makes man the equal of Angels, pleasing to God, terrible to devils, and a model for all the faithful. How enviable, how desirable is the service of God! By it we earn the sum of all that is good, and the joy with which our service is rewarded is one that will have no end.

Chapter 11

ON THE NEED TO SIFT AND GOVERN
THE DESIRES OF THE HEART

The Beloved: My son, there are still a good many things you need to learn, things that up to now you have not learned properly.—What things do you mean, Lord?—These: to make your desires wholly in accordance with my good pleasure, to stop being a lover of yourself, and to become instead a zealous doer of my will. Often you feel within you the flame of desire, urging you insistently forward; but you ought to consider which motive spurs you the more—my honour, or your own advantage. If it is on my account that you act, you will be perfectly happy, however I make things turn out; if, on the other hand, there is a certain amount of self-interest concealed among your motives, you have something there which you will find a bar and a drag.

2. You must beware, then, of placing overmuch reliance on any preconceived desire of your own, forgetting to ask my advice. You might regret it later on and come to dislike what at first took your fancy, something you were eager for as being a change for the better. You must not immediately follow the lead of every feeling that you consider good; on the other hand, a feeling that runs counter to your own leanings is not to be rejected out of hand. It's a good thing to use the curb now and then, even on inclinations and desires good in themselves; otherwise, if they are not kept within reasonable limits, you may find that your mind is being pulled in various directions at once; others may find your want of control a bar to their spiritual progress; and if people start opposing you, you may even get thrown suddenly off your balance, and down you will come.

3. There are times when you have to get tough, and play the man, going dead against your sensual appetite and not caring what the body likes or what it doesn't, but making sure that despite its protests it gives in to the spirit. It must

be corrected and made to serve you, until it is ready for anything, until it learns to be content with little and not to grumble at anything not to its liking.

Chapter 12

ON ACQUIRING PATIENCE
AND BATTLING AGAINST EVIL DESIRES

The Learner: Lord God, I can see that patience is something vitally necessary to me, because this life abounds in circumstances that thwart our happiness. No matter how carefully I endeavour to live in peace, my days must have their share of conflict and sorrow.

2. *The Beloved:* That is so, my son; but the kind of peace I want you to aim at is not one in which temptations are not present, or difficulties not felt. The time when you may reckon you have found peace is when you have been harassed by various temptations and put to the proof by much adversity. If you say you cannot stand much suffering, how are you going to stand the fire of purgatory? You should always choose the lesser of two evils. To escape eternal punishment in the world to come, you should strive to bear patiently for God's sake the evils of this present life. Do you suppose worldly men have next to nothing in the way of suffering? Put the question to those whose lives are a round of pleasures; you will find you are wrong.

3. All the same, you say, they have a lot of fun and follow their own sweet will, so that when they do come up against trouble it doesn't weigh very heavily upon them.

4. Granted; but even supposing they have whatever they desire, how long do you think that's going to last? Those rich in this world's goods, you know, will fade out like smoke, leave not a memory behind of the pleasures that once were theirs. Even during their lifetime, when such pleasures are the goal of their existence, their enjoyment of

them is tinged with bitterness, boredom and fear. The very objects from which they obtain pleasure often repay them with pain and unhappiness. In this they are only getting their due; those who throw off all restraint in their pursuit of pleasure cannot expect to enjoy it without feelings of shame, without finding the sweetness of it turning sour to the taste. Ah, how quickly gone, how false such pleasures are, how uncontrolled, how vile! And yet their devotees are so fuddled by them, so blinded, they fail to see the way they are going; like dumb beasts, they snatch at the paltry pleasures of this corruptible life, and so bring upon themselves the death of their souls. Do you, then, my son, *not follow the counsel of appetite; turn your back on your own liking.*[1] *Let all your longing be fixed in the Lord; so he will give you what your heart desires.*[2]

5. If you would know what true pleasure is, if you long for a greater outpouring of my comfort, I tell you this: despise all worldly things, cut out of your life all base forms of pleasure, and you will be blessed for it, be more than repaid by the comfort with which I shall flood your heart. The more you withdraw from the comfort you find in anything created, the sweeter and stronger will be the comfort you find in me. To begin with, you will not reach this state without a hard struggle and a certain amount of pain. Lifelong habits will bar the way, but better ones will wrest the victory from them. The body will complain, but fervour of spirit will hold it in check. The Old Serpent will goad you and work upon your feelings, but prayer will put him to flight; moreover, by taking up some useful kind of work you will be blocking one of his broadest means of access to your heart.

[1] Ecclus. 18. 30.   [2] Ps. 36. 4.

Chapter 13

ON HUMBLE OBEDIENCE,
AFTER THE EXAMPLE OF JESUS CHRIST

The Beloved: My son, the man who tries breaking away from obedience is breaking away from grace; by seeking benefits for yourself alone, you lose those which are shared by all. When a man does not freely and willingly submit to his superior, it is a sign that the bodily side of him is not yet completely under control, but is kicking back at him and having a grumble. If you want to subdue your animal nature, then, you must learn to obey your superior without delay; the foes who assail you from without are sooner overcome if there has been no ravaging of our inmost self. Your soul has no worse enemy, none more troublesome, than you yourself, when you are out of harmony with the spirit. If you want to win the mastery over flesh and blood, it is of paramount necessity for you to acquire a real contempt for yourself. You are still over-fond of yourself in the wrong kind of way; that is why you flinch from submitting yourself wholly to the will of others.

2. What is so wonderful about your submitting to man for God's sake, you who are but dust and nothingness? Did not I, the Almighty, the Most High, who made all things from nothing, humbly submit to man for your sake? I became the lowliest and least of men, that by my humility I might crush your pride. Here is a lesson in obedience for you, O creature of dust. You that are but earth and slime, learn how to humble yourself, to bow down beneath the feet of all. Learn how to break your own will and to surrender yourself in complete submission.

3. Direct the fire of your anger against yourself; do not let pride, that monstrous growth, draw nourishment from you any more; but shew yourself so submissive, so unimportant, that everyone may walk over you, trample you like mud in the streets. And if they do, what reason have you to complain, you worthless man? Filthy sinner that you are,

what answer can you make to those who reproach you, you who have so often offended God, so many a time deserved hell? And yet my pity spared you, because your soul was precious in my sight; I wanted you to come to the knowledge of my love, to be ever grateful for my kindness towards you; to give yourself unceasingly to true submission and humility, and to bear with patience the scorn of others.

Chapter 14

ON THE NEED TO CONSIDER THE SECRET JUDGEMENTS OF GOD; A WARNING AGAINST BEING VAIN OF OUR GOOD QUALITIES

The Learner: Lord, when the thunder of your judgements peals out above me, every bone in my body shakes with fear and trembling, and my soul is aghast with terror. There I stand, dazed with dread, as I consider that the very heavens are not pure in your sight. You found evil among the Angels, and yet you did not spare them; then what will become of me? The very stars fell from heaven; what hope dare I have, I who am but dust? Men whose deeds appeared worthy of praise have fallen to the lowest depths; men who ate the Bread of Angels I have seen feeding with relish on pigs' garbage.

2. There can be no holiness, then, Lord, if you withdraw your supporting hand. No wisdom can be of any help, once you cease to guide it; no courage can support us, if you cease to keep it in being. No chastity is secure when you are not its guardian. No watch we keep by ourselves can avail us, if you do not keep holy vigil at our side. No, when you leave us, we sink and perish; when you visit us, we are raised up and restored to life. We have no sure footing, but through you we are made firm; we grow cold at heart, but you stir us once more into flame.

3. I ought to think of myself as the least and most un-

important of men; and if I *do* seem to have any good points about me, I ought to reckon them as nothing. How deeply, Lord, must I submit myself to your unsearchable judgements! In those bottomless depths what do I find myself to be? Nothing, just nothing. You are greatness beyond all measure, an ocean to whose further shore none may ever sail; in you I find myself to be nothing, utterly nothing. What place is there here for pride to lurk in? Where now is my confidence in my store of virtue? All my empty self-approval is swallowed up in the depths of your judgements upon me.

4. What is all flesh in your sight? "Shall the clay dare ask the potter who moulds it, What ails you?" How can a man extol himself with empty boasting, if his heart is truly subject to God? The whole world cannot make a man put himself on a pedestal if the Truth has made him subject to itself; the man who has fixed his whole hope in God will not be moved by the lips of all who praise him. Why, all those who so praise him are themselves nothing; they will vanish along with the sound of their words; but *the Lord remains faithful to his word for ever.*[1]

Chapter 15

ON THE WAY WE OUGHT TO ACT AND PRAY
WITH REGARD TO OUR DESIRES

The Beloved: My son, this is how you should pray in all circumstances: "Lord, if this is what pleases you, let it come to pass. Lord, if this will be to your honour, let it happen in your name. Lord, if you see this to be for my good, if you judge it to be profitable for me, give me this thing to use for your honour; but if you foresee it will do me harm, impair the health of my soul, take away from me the desire for such a thing." Not every desire comes from the

[1] Ps. 116. 2.

Holy Ghost, even though to man it may seem good and upright. It's not so easy to tell for certain if it's a good spirit or an evil one urging you to desire this thing or that; it may be only the prompting of your own spirit. Many people have ended by being deceived; yet when they began it looked as if they had a good spirit for their guide.

2. So, then, whenever the thought comes into your mind that such and such a thing is desirable, you must always desire it, pray for it, in the fear of God and with a humble heart; above all, you must renounce your own ideas about the matter and leave it entirely to me, saying: "Lord, you know which way is for the best; let it happen this way or that, according as you will. Give what you will, in whatever measure you will, and when you will. Do with me as you know is best, as pleases you best, and as will best promote your glory. Put me where you will and have a free hand with me in everything. Yes, I am in your hand; twist me around and turn me about as you will. I am your servant, and ready for anything; it is not for myself that I want to live, but for you. If only I could do that worthily and faultlessly!"

A Prayer that we may do what God wants of us

3. O most kind Jesus, give me your grace, to be at my side too, and share my labours, to be my constant companion to the end. Grant that I may always will and desire what is more acceptable to you, whatever pleases you more dearly. Let your will be mine, let mine ever follow yours in perfect harmony. Let my wishes and dislikes be identical with yours; let me be unable to wish or dislike anything that you do not wish or dislike.

4. Grant that I may die to all that is in the world and for your sake love to be scorned and unknown in this earthly life. Grant that in you, above all the things I desire, I may find rest, that only in you my heart may be at peace. You are the heart's true peace, you alone can give it rest; all that is outside you is hard and never still. In that selfsame

107

peace, in you who are the one, supreme and eternal good, *even as I lie down, sleep comes, and with sleep tranquillity.*[1] Amen.

Chapter 16

TRUE COMFORT SHOULD BE SOUGHT IN GOD ALONE

The Learner: Whatever I can desire, whatever my thoughts can conceive in the way of comfort, I look to find not here, but later on. Even though I alone had all the comforts of the world, even though I could revel in all its pleasures, they could not last for long, that's certain. That is why my soul will never be able to find fullness of comfort, never be perfectly refreshed, save only in God, the comforter of the poor and refuge of the humble. Wait but a little while, my soul, wait for God to keep his promise, and in heaven you will have good things of all kinds, overflowing the cup of his bounty. But if you are full of uncontrolled yearning for the good things of this present life, you will lose those which belong to heaven and eternal life. Let the things of time be for you to use, but those of eternity the goal of your longings. None of the good things of this world can satisfy you; it was not to enjoy them alone that you were created.

2. Even though you possessed every good thing God has made, it could not make you happy and blessed; no, it is in God, who made all these things, that your whole blessedness lies, your whole happiness. I don't mean the kind of happiness envisaged by those foolish enough to love the world, the kind that earns their approval; no, I mean that happiness to which good and faithful followers of Christ look forward, that happiness of which a foretaste is sometimes given to the spiritual and the pure in heart, whose earthly lives are spent in heaven. All the comfort we get from human sources is empty and soon gone; true comfort,

[1] Ps. 4. 9.

blessed comfort, is that which is inwardly given by the Truth. A devout man, wherever he may be, takes everywhere with him his comforter, Jesus, and says to him: "Be with me, Lord Jesus, at every moment and in every place." Let this, then, be my comfort, my willingness to forgo all comfort that comes from man; and if I do not receive your comfort, let my highest comfort be the thought that it is by your will, your justice, that I am thus being tested; because *he will not always be finding fault, his frown does not last for ever.*[1]

Chapter 17

WE MUST PUT OUR WHOLE TRUST IN GOD

The Beloved: My son, let me do with you as I will; I know what is best for you. It is but as a man that you think; your feelings in many matters are swayed by the human way of looking at things.

The Learner: Lord, they are true, those words of yours. Your watchfulness on my behalf is greater than any care I could take of myself. A man stands in great danger of falling, if he does not put his whole trust in you. Lord, do with me whatever you please, if only my will may stay fixed on you, without weakening or wavering; whatever you do with me, it cannot but be good, because it is your doing.

2. If you wish me to be in darkness, bless you, Lord; if you wish me to be in light, bless you again. If you in your mercy comfort me, bless you; and if you want me to pass through trouble, bless you just the same.

3. *The Beloved:* My son, that is the stand you must take, if you would walk beside me. You should be as ready to suffer as to be happy, as willing to be poor and needy as rich and well supplied.

4. *The Learner:* Lord, I will gladly bear for your sake

[1] Ps. 102. 9.

whatever you will to befall me. I wish to accept from your hand good and bad alike, sweet and sour, happiness and sorrow, and to thank you for all that happens to me. Keep me from all sin, and I shall fear neither death nor hell. Whatever troubles come upon me, they will do me no harm, if only you do not cast me off for ever, do not scratch out my name from the book of life.

Chapter 18

WE MUST FOLLOW CHRIST IN BEARING
PATIENTLY THE SORROWS OF LIFE

The Beloved: My son, I came down from heaven to save you. I took your sorrows upon me; I had no need to do so, but my love for you drew me on. The lesson I wanted you to learn was that of patience, of bearing the sorrows of life without bitterness. From the hour of my birth until my death upon the cross, there was never a moment when I had no sorrow to bear. My store of worldly goods amounted to very little; many and frequent were the complaints I heard people make about me; when they shamed and insulted me I took it gently. My kindnesses were repaid with ingratitude, my miracles with blasphemy, my teachings with rebuke.

2. *The Learner:* Lord, during your life you were patient, thereby fulfilling to the utmost the bidding of your Father; it is only right, then, that I, a mere wretched sinner, should bear things patiently, in accordance with your will, and to save my soul shoulder for as long as you will the load of this corruptible life. We feel the weight of this present life; yet through your grace it has become the source of great merit; and your own example, and the steps your Saints have trodden, have made it easier for the weak to endure, and greater in glory. It is a life much richer in consolation than it was in former times, under the Old Law. Then the gate of heaven stayed shut, and even the road to it seemed

unsure, since there were so few at that time who cared to look for the kingdom of heaven. And even the holy men of those days, those due to be saved, could not enter the kingdom of heaven until by your passion and your holy death you had paid their debt for them.

3. What a debt of gratitude I owe you, for your mercy in shewing me, along with all your faithful followers, the straight and true road that leads to your eternal kingdom! That road we must follow is your own life; by holy patience we make our way towards you, you who are to crown our journey. Had you not gone before and shewn us the way, which of us would care to follow it? Many, I fear, would stay behind, remain at a distance, if they had not your wondrous example to gaze at. Why, even now, for all the times we have heard of your teaching and all your miracles, the flame within us burns low; what would happen if we lacked that great glow of light to guide us in following you?

Chapter 19

ON BEARING INJURIES, AND HOW
TO TELL WHEN YOU ARE REALLY PATIENT

The Beloved: What is that you are saying, my son? Think how much I have suffered, I and my Saints, and stop complaining. *Your protest, your battle against sin, has not yet called for bloodshed.*[1] What you have to put up with is little enough, compared with those who have borne so much, been so strongly tempted, so grievously tried, sifted and tested in so many ways.

You should call to mind the much heavier sufferings of others; that will make you bear your own little miseries with a lighter heart. Perhaps to you they don't look so very little; if so, see whether it isn't your unwillingness to suffer which is magnifying them for you. In any case, whether your

[1] Heb. 12. 4.

troubles are little or great, try to bear them all with patience.

2. The better disposed you are to accept suffering, the more wisely you are acting, and the greater is the merit you are earning; you will find things easier to bear if you have not been idle in preparing yourself for suffering by getting your mind used to the idea. Don't say, "I can't let So-and-so treat me like that; I really can't put up with that kind of thing. He has got me into serious trouble, charging me with doing things that had never even entered my head. If it were anybody else, I wouldn't mind; I'd just let it pass as one of those things you have to put up with." That's a silly way of thinking; you are forgetting that patience is a virtue, forgetting who will reward you for practising it; all you can think of is the person concerned and the wrong he has done you.

3. A man is not really patient when he is willing to suffer patiently only as much as he thinks fit and only at the hands of those he chooses. If he is really patient, he won't mind who makes him suffer; his superior, his equal or someone below him, a good, holy man or a peevish, unpleasant one— it's all the same to him. Whenever things go against him, no matter how often or how gravely, no matter who or what is at the back of it, he takes it all thankfully from the hand of God, counting it as a substantial gain; because in the eyes of God no trouble endured for his sake, be it never so trivial, can be allowed to go by without earning merit.

4. If you want to gain the victory, then, be ready for battle; you can't win the crown of patience without having a fight. If you refuse to suffer, you are refusing that crown; but if you desire to be crowned, fight like a man and hold out in patience. There's no attaining rest without toil, no reaching victory without a battle.

5. *The Learner:* Lord, let what seems impossible for me to do by nature become possible by your grace. You know how little I can stand, how soon I lose heart at the least little bit of trouble. Let every trial and affliction become, for your name's sake, something to be loved and desired; because suffering and affliction for your sake is the best of medicines for my soul.

Chapter 20

ON ACKNOWLEDGING OUR OWN WEAKNESS
AND ON THE MISERIES OF THIS LIFE

The Learner: Lord, I will tell you frankly, and to my shame, how sinful I am, how weak. It's often something quite trivial that upsets me and throws me out of balance. I make up my mind to take a firm line in the matter, and then, the moment the slightest temptation comes along, I find myself in a very tight corner. It's sometimes something quite petty that gives rise to a really serious temptation; I'm feeling fairly safe, and then, before I know what's happening, I sometimes find myself almost knocked over by the lightest gust.

2. So you see, Lord, how wretchedly frail I am; everything in the world will have told you that. Have pity on me; "save me from sinking in the mire"; don't let me stay down all the time. That is what often distresses me and shames me in your sight; that I am so apt to fall, so weak in resisting my passions. Even though I don't give way to them altogether, the way they keep on at me all the time is very irksome and distressing; I get sick and tired of living day in, day out, at war with myself. All this shews me how weak I am; the most loathsome fancies always rush in upon me much more readily than they take their leave.

3. Most powerful God of Israel, passionate lover of faithful souls, look upon the toil and trouble of this servant of yours; stand by him in all he sets his hand to. Strengthen me with heavenly courage; otherwise, the man I was once by nature, the wretched flesh not yet fully subject to the spirit, may be strong enough to overcome me. It is against this that I shall have to struggle so long as I draw breath in this sorry life. And oh, what a life it is! One long series of troubles and miseries, everything full of hidden traps and enemies! As soon as one trial or temptation takes itself off, along comes another; and while the first battle is still on, up come several more, out of the blue.

113

4. How can people love life, riddled as it is with bitterness, the prey of so many disasters and miseries? The very word "life" is surely a misnomer for something so prolific in death and misery. And yet it is loved, and there are many who seek all their pleasures from it. The world is often blamed for being deceitful and vain; yet it is not readily given up—fleshly desires have far too strong a say. There are some things that lead men to love the world, others that move them to despise it. The things that lead men to love the world are *gratification of corrupt nature, gratification of the eye, the empty pomp of living*,[1] but the penalties and miseries that rightly follow in the wake of these things fill men with disgust and hatred of the world.

5. But the sorry fact is that a distorted notion of pleasure conquers the mind that has surrendered to the world; it deems that enjoyment is to be found underlying the senses. The reason for this is that it has neither seen nor tasted the sweetness of God and the inward delight of holiness. But those who utterly despise the world and strive to live for God under a holy rule of life, are far from being unaware of that divine sweetness promised to all who really do renounce the world. They see more clearly than other men how sorely the world is astray, how manifold are its departures from the truth.

Chapter 21

WE MUST REST IN GOD
ABOVE ALL HIS GIFTS AND FAVOURS

The Learner: My soul, above all things and in all things you must always rest in the Lord, for he is the everlasting rest of the Saints. O sweetest, most loving Jesus, grant that I may rest in you above anything created; above all health and beauty, all honour and glory; above all power and dig-

[1] 1 John 2. 16.

nity, all knowledge and cleverness; above all riches and abilities; above all joy and gladness, above all fame and praise; above all sweetness and consolation; above all hope and promise, above all merit and desire; above all gifts and presents you can give us or pour out upon us; above all happiness and rejoicing that the mind can grasp and feel; finally, above Angels and Archangels and above the whole host of heaven; above everything seen or unseen, above everything that is not you, my God.

2. O Lord my God, you are the sum of all good, surpassing all things; you alone are most high and most powerful; you alone are completely self-sufficient and perfect; you alone are most sweet and consoling. You alone are most beautiful and most loving, most noble and most glorious above all else; in you are found existing together in all their perfection all good things that now are or ever have been or ever will be. Thus it is that anything you give me apart from yourself, anything you reveal or promise me of yourself, is too little, too unsatisfying, for as yet I have not seen you, have not fully gained possession of you. My heart cannot find its true resting-place, cannot be wholly content, until it soars above all your gifts, all that you have created, and rests in you.

3. O Jesus Christ, my dearest spouse, my lover of stainless purity, ruler of the whole creation: who will give me wings of true freedom, that I may fly to you and in you take my rest? When will it be granted to me in full to have nothing to do but see how sweet you are, O Lord my God? When may I be wholly absorbed in you, that for very love of you I may be unaware of myself, may know only you, above all the ways we know through our senses, in a fashion not known to all? But now, how often I sigh, as I bear with grief my load of unhappiness! Many are the evils I meet with in this vale of sorrows; often they trouble me, sadden me, befog my path; often hinder and distract me, lure and entangle me, to prevent me from coming to you freely, from knowing the bliss of your embrace, which for the blessed spirits is an ever-present joy. Let my sighing touch your

115

heart; in so many ways am I a lonely outcast upon earth!

4. O Jesus, brightness of the everlasting glory, comfort of the soul on its pilgrimage here, my lips beseech you without sound of words, my silence speaks to you. How much longer will my Lord delay his coming? I am but little and poor, but let him come to me and make me glad; let him stretch out his hand and rescue a poor wretch from all the troubles that fence him in. Ah, come, come! Without you, not a day is happy, not a single hour! You are my happiness; without you, there is no one to share my table. I am full of misery, something like a prisoner with his burden of fetters, until you cheer me with the light of your presence, give me back my freedom, and turn towards me the face of a friend.

5. Let others seek instead of you whatever takes their fancy; for me, there is nothing that gives me such joy, nor ever will be, but you, my God, my hope, my eternal salvation. I will not keep quiet, not cease to beg for your favour, until your grace returns and I hear your voice within me once more.

6. *The Beloved:* Here I am; see, I have come to you, because you called for me. Your tears, and the longing in your soul, your being humbled, your crushed and broken heart, have moved me and brought me to you.

7. Lord, I called for you in my longing to enjoy your dear company; for your sake I am ready to give up all else. It was you who first moved me to seek you; bless you, Lord, for doing your servant this kindness in your unbounded mercy. What more can your servant say to you? He can only lie in utter abasement before you, ever conscious of his own sinfulness and unimportance. Yes, there is nothing to compare with you out of all the wonders of heaven and earth. All your works are good, all your judgements are true; your providence is at the helm of all creation. Let praise and glory be yours, then, O Wisdom of the Father; let my lips, my soul and the whole of creation together praise you and bless you.

Chapter 22

ON RECALLING GOD'S MANIFOLD BLESSINGS

The Learner: Lord, open this heart of mine and place your law within it; teach me to walk by the road of your commandments. Grant that I may know what your will is; grant that my mind may dwell with great reverence and careful attention upon all your blessings, both those common to all men and those which are your gift to me; so may I be enabled to thank you in future as you deserve. Yet I know and confess that I am unable to praise and thank you as I ought, even for the very least of your favours. I am much less than all the blessings you have showered upon me; when I realize how infinitely high you are above your creation, my mind whirls at the thought of your greatness.

2. All qualities of soul and body that are ours, whatever we possess, inwardly or outwardly, naturally or supernaturally, come from your bounty; they shew us how bounteous you are, how loving, how good, you from whom we have received all these blessings. Some may have been given more, some less, but all alike come from you, and without you we could not have even the least of them. The man who has received a larger share cannot boast of it as being won by his own merit, cannot affect a superior attitude towards others or treat as dirt those less gifted than himself; the less a man attributes his good qualities to himself, the more humble and devout the thanks he gives to God for them, a greater man, a better man, is he. The man who ranks himself below all others and counts himself unworthy of God's favour is better fitted for receiving that favour in greater measure.

3. If a man has been given but few gifts, it should not make him unhappy; he oughtn't to be bitter about it or envy those more lavishly endowed. Instead, he should turn to you and give you his highest praise for your goodness in bestowing your gifts so generously, so freely, so willingly, without respect of persons. It is from you that all things

come; it is right, therefore, that in all things you should be praised. You know what gifts are best suited to each one of us; you know why one man has less and another more. That is not for us to judge, but for you, who can assess the merits of every man alive.

4. That being so, I count it a great favour, Lord God, not to have many of those qualities which, as outward things go and to man's way of thinking, appear to confer honour and glory on their owner. When a man reflects upon his poverty and insignificance, it should not make him low-spirited or unhappy or depressed; no, it should make him feel consoled and full of joy, because it is just such poor and humble folk that you have chosen, my God, to be your close friends and servants. Your own Apostles are a proof of this choice of yours; you caused them to *divide a world between them for their domains.*[1] Yet they lived uncomplaining lives upon earth, so unassuming and simple, so innocent of malice and double-dealing that they even *rejoiced that they had been found worthy to suffer indignity for your name's sake;*[2] and with great ardour embraced what the world shrinks from in fear.

5. Thus, when a man loves you and knows your kindnesses towards him, nothing should give him greater joy than the accomplishing in him of your will, and the good pleasure of your eternal purpose. So contented this ought to make him, so full of comfort, that he would as readily be the least of men as another might long to be the greatest. He should be as much contented and at peace in the lowest place as in the highest, as willing to be considered a person nobody wants, a target for sneers, a complete nonentity, as to be greater and more respected than the rest of men. Your will, and the desire of upholding your honour, should come before everything else; these will bring greater comfort, greater pleasure, than all the blessings a man has been given, or might hope to receive.

[1] Ps. 44. 16.   [2] Acts 5. 41.

118

Chapter 23

ON FOUR THINGS THAT BRING GREAT PEACE

The Beloved: Now, my son, I will shew you the path of peace and true freedom.

2. *The Learner:* Do as you say, Lord: that is something I should be glad to hear about.

3. *The Beloved:* My son, always try to do the will of others rather than your own. Always choose to have less rather than more; always make for the lowest place and take rank below all others. Let your constant prayer and desire be that the will of God may be perfectly accomplished in you. The man who does all this crosses the frontier of the land of peace and inward rest.

4. *The Learner:* Lord, those few words of yours hold within them the highroad to perfection; they do not take long to say, but they are full of meaning and rich in results. If I could only keep them faithfully, it would not be so easy for me to lose my peace of mind. Every time I am conscious of feeling restless and heavy-hearted, I find I have been going against this teaching of yours. However, there is nothing beyond your power, and you love to see a soul making headway; so give me, Lord, a greater store of your grace, to enable me to keep your word and ensure my salvation.

A Prayer against Evil Thoughts

5. O Lord my God, do not go far away from me; look upon me, my God, and help me, for swarming thoughts have broken out in rebellion against me, together with deep fears that harass my soul. How am I to pass through them without getting a wound? How am I to break my way through them?

6. Of old you said: *I will still lead you on your way, bending the pride of earth low before you.*[1] I will open the gates

[1] Isaias 45. 2.

119

of the prison, and shew you the mysteries of the secret places.

7. Lord, do as you have said: let all evil thoughts flee at the sight of you. This is my hope, my one comfort, that in all my troubles I can turn to you, trust you, call upon you from the depths of my being, and in patience wait for you to comfort me.

A Prayer for Light to shine in our Mind

8. O good Jesus, let the brightness of your inward light shine clearly within my mind; banish all darkness from the house of my heart. Fence in my many roving thoughts and crush the temptations that use such force against me. Fight on my side with all your strength and overcome those evil beasts, the fleshly lusts that lure me to wrong; so will your power bring peace, and the mighty sound of your praise ring out in that holy temple, a conscience free from stain. Give your commands to the winds and to the storms; bid the sea to be calm and the blustering wind not to blow, and there shall be a great stillness.

9. Send forth your light and your truth to shine upon the earth; I myself am but earth, empty and waste, until you shed your light upon me. Pour down your grace from above; soak my heart with the rain of heaven; bring me streams of devotion to water the face of this earth, to make it bear good and perfect fruit. Take from my mind the load of sin that weighs so heavily upon it, and fix all my desires upon the things of heaven, so that, once I have tasted the sweetness of that joy above, I may be loth to let my thoughts dwell on the things of earth.

10. Catch hold of me and drag me away from the comfort to be found in things created, a comfort that cannot last; for there is nothing in all creation that can fully slake my longings, fully give me comfort. Bind me to you with a bond of love that cannot be broken; for you alone are all-in-all for a loving heart, and without you everything else is but pitiful trash.

Chapter 24

ON AVOIDING CURIOSITY
ABOUT THE LIVES OF OTHERS

The Beloved: My son, you must not always be indulging your curiosity and concerning yourself with things that don't matter. This affair or that—what have they to do with you? Your business is to follow me. What difference does it make to you whether So-and-so has one kind of character or another, whether someone else behaves or speaks in this way or that? You are not required to answer for others, but you will have to give an account of your own life, so why mix yourself up in the affairs of others? See here, I know all men and see all that goes on beneath the sun; I know how things stand with every single man—what he thinks of, what his desires are, and the goal of his intentions. So leave everything in my hands, and allow nothing to disturb your peace of mind. As for your restless talebearer, let him gossip away as much as he likes; all those words and deeds of his will come back to accuse him; he cannot deceive me.

2. Do not be anxious to bask in the favour of the great and famous, to have a large circle of acquaintances, to enjoy the particular affection of certain men; these things are a breeding-ground of distractions, and fill the heart with great darkness. Would you but keep careful watch for my coming, and open to me the door of your heart, I would gladly speak to you and lift the veil from my secrets. Be wary, keep watch by praying, and in all things be humble.

Chapter 25

ON SURE PEACE OF MIND AND TRUE PROGRESS

The Beloved: This is what I said once, my son: *Peace is my bequest to you, and the peace which I will give you is mine to give; I do not give peace as the world gives it.*[1] Peace is something everyone longs for, but it is not everyone who troubles to find out what brings true peace. My peace is to be found among those who are humble and gentle of heart; you will find your own peace in the practice of great patience. If you listen to me and follow my words, you will be able to enjoy great peace of mind.

2. *The Learner:* Well then, what must I do?

3. *The Beloved:* You must at all times pay attention to what you do and what you say, and make it your constant aim to please me alone, desiring and seeking nothing apart from myself. Do not make rash judgements on what other people say or do, and do not involve yourself in matters which are no concern of yours. Keep these rules, and you will have little to trouble your mind, and that but seldom. You must not expect, though, never to feel disquieted, never to suffer grief of heart or bodily pain; such freedom from trouble belongs not to this present life but to the life of eternal rest. So don't go thinking you have found true peace, just because you feel no heaviness of heart; don't imagine all is well with you, because no one happens to be thwarting you for the moment; and don't imagine you have reached perfection simply because everything turns out just as you want it. Even when you experience great devotion and inward sweetness, you must not think yourself a privileged person, one of God's close friends; it isn't by things like this that the true lover of holiness is known; such things are no sign of a man's spiritual progress and perfection.

4. *The Learner:* What *are* these signs, then, Lord?

5. *The Beloved:* Surrendering yourself with all your heart to the will of God; never seeking your own will, whether

[1] John 14. 27.

in great things or little, in time or in eternity; being steadfast in this attitude, so that, whether things go well with you or otherwise, you go on thanking God in just the same way, letting nothing, good or bad, upset the even balance of your heart. If you have the courage, the unfaltering hope, tó steel your heart to bear even heavier trials, when you have lost all inward comfort; if you do not complain of the injustice of your lot, as if it were not right for you to undergo such great suffering, but acknowledge the justice of all my dealings with you, and praise my holy name: you may know then that you are walking on the true and unswerving path of peace, and nothing will be able to shake your hope of seeing my face once more in joy. If you reach that state in which you have nothing but contempt for yourself, you can be sure you are enjoying the greatest measure of peace possible for you during your stay upon earth.

Chapter 26

ON THE EXCELLENCE OF A FREE MIND, THE REWARD OF HUMBLE PRAYER RATHER THAN OF READING

The Learner: Lord, it is the business of a man of perfect life never to loosen the bonds that bind his heart to heavenly things; to make his way through a crowd of troubles as if he had no trouble at all, not like someone too stupid to be alive to his plight but in the privileged possession of a free mind that clings to nothing in creation with ill-regulated affection.

2. O most loving God, I beg you to keep me from the cares of this life, so that I may not become too closely involved in them; from the many needs of the body, for fear of the snares of pleasure; from everything that blocks the way my soul would go, that I may not be overwhelmed by my troubles and become downcast. I do not ask to be kept from those things that are pursued so whole-heartedly

by the frivolous and the worldly, but from those miseries which weigh so heavily, so painfully, upon the soul of your servant, who shares in the curse pronounced on mortal man in general, miseries that hold him back from entering into spiritual freedom as often as he would like to.

3. O my God, you who are sweetness surpassing all speech, turn sour for me the taste of any bodily comfort that draws me away from the love of eternal things, enticing me, to my hurt, by the sight of some pleasure to be enjoyed in this present life. Do not let them overcome me, my God, do not let them overcome me, this flesh and blood of mine; let me not be deceived by the world and its fleeting glory; do not let the Devil and his wiles trip me by the heels. Give me strength to resist, patience to hold out, steadfastness to keep going until the end. Give me the sweet balm of your spirit instead of all the delights of the world; empty my heart of fleshly love and fill it instead with the love of your name.

4. To a fervent spirit, having to make use of food, drink, clothing and other things to keep the body going is a burden; grant that I may be sparing in my use of such bodily comforts and not over-anxious to enjoy them. It is not right to dispense with them entirely; we have to make provision for the needs of our nature; but your holy law forbids us to seek for unnecessary luxuries. Otherwise, if we did, the flesh would rise in revolt against the spirit. In all these matters, I pray that I may be guided and directed by your hand, so as to avoid extravagance.

Chapter 27

SELF-LOVE IS A GREAT HINDRANCE
IN OUR QUEST FOR THE HIGHEST GOOD

The Beloved: My son, you must give me all for all, keep no aspect of yourself as your private concern. You know, loving yourself does you more harm than anything in the world. The hold which anything has upon your heart is determined by the love and affection you bear towards that thing. If your love is sincere, simple and under control you will not be held prisoner by things. Do not desire what it is not right for you to have, or possess anything that may get in your way and deprive you of inward freedom. How strange it is that you do not trust yourself to me from the bottom of your heart, together with all that you can desire or possess.

2. Why waste away in useless grief, why wear yourself out with unnecessary cares? Wait on my good pleasure, and you shall come to no harm. If you want this thing or that, or have a mind to be in one place or another, to gratify your own taste or convenience, you will never be at rest, never free from care; in everything you will find some lack of perfection, in every place someone to thwart your wishes.

3. There is nothing to be gained, then, by acquiring and increasing outward possessions; what *does* do you good is to think nothing of such things, cut them right out of your hearts, root and branch. I am speaking not only of amassing riches but also of going about in quest of honours and of the desire to receive vain praise. All these things pass away together with the world. The place you live in can be but a poor defence, if you lack fervour of spirit; if you seek for peace in outward affairs it will not stay firm for long, if your heart is not standing on its proper foundations, on me, I mean. You can find somewhere else to live in, but it will not make you any better; the chance may come, and you accept it; but even there you will find what you were trying to get away from, and probably worse troubles into the bargain.

A Prayer for a Clean Heart
and Heavenly Wisdom

4. O God, strengthen me by the grace of your Holy Spirit. Make firm within me my efforts to be holy; empty my heart of all unnecessary worry and anxiety, and do not let it be carried away by the desire of anything whatsoever,

125

whether worth the having or otherwise. Make me see that all things are passing away, and that I, too, must one day follow them; for there is nothing beneath the sun that lasts for ever, and everything here is *but frustration and lost labour, all of it.*[1] He is a wise man whose thoughts run thus.

5. Lord, give me your heavenly wisdom, that I may learn to seek you and find you above all things else, to love and understand you more than anything; let me see all other things as they are, in the way your wisdom has disposed them. Give me the prudence to keep away from those who flatter me, the patience to bear with those who oppose me. This is wisdom indeed, to refuse to be swayed by every gust of speech from the mouths of men, and not to give ear to those Siren voices that lure a man so sweetly to his doom. Following such a course, we advance fearlessly along the road we have begun to tread.

Chapter 28

AGAINST SLANDEROUS TALK

The Beloved: You must not mind, my son, if people think ill of you and say things about you which do not make pleasant hearing. You ought to have a poorer opinion of yourself than they have, and deem no one to be weaker than yourself. If you are treading the path of the inward life, fleeting words will not carry much weight with you. It is a wise course, when trouble comes, to say nothing, and to turn inwardly to me, refusing to be upset by what men think about you.

2. You must not let your peace of mind depend on what people say about you. The construction they put on your actions may be correct or false; that doesn't make a different man of you. Where will you find true peace, real glory? It is in me, as you well know. The man who is neither bent

[1] Eccles. 1. 14.

126

upon pleasing his fellows nor afraid of offending them will enjoy great peace. It is from affections allowed to run wild and from baseless fears that all disquiet of heart arises, all distraction of the feelings.

Chapter 29

HOW WE SHOULD CALL ON GOD AND BLESS HIM WHEN TROUBLE THREATENS

The Learner: Lord, may your name be blessed for ever; it is by your will that this trouble and temptation have come upon me. I cannot get out of it, but I must come to you for protection, that you may help me and make it turn out for my good. Lord, I am in trouble at the moment; there is no peace in my heart, but I am much disturbed by this affliction now pressing on me. What can I say now, my beloved Father? I am trapped in a tight place. *Save me from undergoing this hour of trial.*[1] Yet that is why I have come to this hour, to bring you the glory of setting me free from this pit of humiliation. Please rescue me, Lord; what can I do, resourceless as I am? Without you, where shall I go? Lord, give me patience, this time also. Help me, my God, and I shall have no fear, no matter how heavy the load I must bear.

2. What shall I say now in the midst of my distress? Lord, may your will be done. I have richly deserved trouble and oppression. I must certainly endure it—patiently, I hope—until the storm blows over and things get better. Your hand is almighty, and has the power to take even this temptation away from me and soften its violence, so that I may not completely give way before it; many a time in the past you have done that for me, my God in your mercy towards me. To me, such a change seems unlikely; that only makes it easier, O God most high, for you to bring it about and lighten my burden.

[1] John 12. 27.

Chapter 30

ON BEGGING GOD'S HELP, AND
BEING CONFIDENT OF RECOVERING HIS GRACE

The Beloved: My son, I am *the Lord; no strength like his in the hour of distress.*[1] When things are not going well with you, come to me. The chief hindrance to your receiving heavenly comfort is your slowness in turning to prayer; you do not come to me straightway and pray to me earnestly, but first you go seeking other things to comfort you, trying to find diversion in created things. All these things, as it happens, do little to help you; it is then that you remember that I am the deliverer of all who put their hope in me; that apart from me there is no help that can do much, no counsel that can be taken with profit, no remedy whose effects can last. But now, when the storm is over and you can breathe freely again, recruit your strength in the light of my mercies; for I am near, I the Lord, to restore all things not only to their former perfection, but to pile them high and make them overflow with added graces.

2. *How should any task be too difficult for me?*[2] Shall I be like a man who promises something and then fails to do it? Where is your faith? Stand firm and hold your ground. Be a man of courage, and wait in patience; my comfort will come to you in its own good time. Watch out for me; yes, watch; I will come and look after you. The trouble that now distresses you is my way of testing you; the fears which fill you with terror have no foundation. What use is it to worry about what the future will bring? It will only make you have sorrow upon sorrow. *For today, today's troubles are enough.*[3] It is silly and useless to get worried or pleasantly excited about future events; quite likely they will never happen at all.

3. Yet it is part of man's make-up to be deceived by picturing things to himself in this way; it is a sign of small spiritual stature when you take to heart so readily whatever your enemy the Devil slips into your mind. He is not par-

[1] Nahum 1. 7   [2] Jer. 32. 27.   [3] Matt. 6. 34.

128

ticular in his choice of tricks to catch you out; truth or falsehood, it's all one to him. So long as he can bring you down, he doesn't mind how he trips you; it may be by making you love the present, or it may be by making you fear the future. So *do not let your heart be distressed, or play the coward!*[1] Trust in me, and have confidence in my mercy. Often, when you feel you are far away from me, I am nearer than you think; when you reckon everything is all but lost, a greater reward for your striving is often just ahead of you. Everything is not lost, just because things are going against you. So don't let your present feelings affect your judgement; and don't cling obstinately to any mood of depression, whatever its origin, letting it settle as though you had lost all hope of ever coming out of it.

4. Don't imagine you have been completely abandoned if I send some trial to afflict you for a while, or if I withdraw from you the comfort you had hoped for; this is the road by which you reach the kingdom of heaven. You may be sure that it is better for you and the rest of my servants to be harassed with things that go against the grain than always to have everything to your liking. I know the thoughts you keep hidden; it is very necessary for your salvation for you to be left now and then without any taste of spiritual sweetness; otherwise, you might start getting conceited ideas about your good progress in the ways of the spirit, and be highly pleased with yourself for reaching a state which is not yet yours. What I have given, I can take away, and restore again when it pleases me to do so.

5. When I give you something, it is still mine; when I take it back, I am not taking anything of yours, because every good gift, every perfect gift, belongs to me. If I send you some affliction or trouble, do not be indignant about it or let it break your heart; I can quickly relieve you of your burden and turn it all into joy. Nevertheless, I am just, and when I so deal with you, you ought to give me all the praise that is my due.

[1] John 14. 27.

129

6. If you are truly wise and see things as they really are, you must never allow troubles to make you unhappy and depressed; no, you should be glad and thank me for them. Indeed, you ought to account it your sole joy that by afflicting you with sorrows I do not spare you. *I have bestowed my love upon you, just as my Father has bestowed his love upon me;*[1] that is what I said to my beloved disciples, and you know what I sent them out to; not to have worldly pleasures, but to fight great battles; not to be honoured, but to be despised; not to have an easy time, but to work hard; not to rest, but to bring forth much fruit in patience. Remember these words of mine, my son.

Chapter 31

ON DISREGARDING CREATURES TO FIND THE CREATOR

The Learner: Lord, I am still much in need of greater grace, if I am to reach that state where no one and nothing in all creation can bar my advance. As long as anything holds me back, I cannot fly freely to you. To fly freely—that was his desire, the man who said, *Had I but wings, I cry, as a dove has wings, to fly away and find rest!*[2] Who is more at rest than the man who is "clear-sighted"? What greater freedom is there than to desire nothing upon earth? A man should therefore rise above all that is created, and, leaving himself completely behind, see with rapt eyes that there is no comparison between creatures and you, the Creator of them all. Unless a man has disentangled himself from all things created, he will not be free to make for the things of God. That is why you find so few contemplatives; there are not so many people who can cut themselves off completely from things created and doomed to pass away.

2. It needs a good deal of grace to lift the soul up so far that it is carried higher than itself; but unless a man is

[1] John 15. 9. [2] Ps. 54. 7.

lifted up in spirit, free of all attachment to creatures and completely united to God, nothing he may know or possess is of much consequence. Anyone who esteems as valuable anything apart from God, the only, the boundless, the eternal good, will long remain small in soul and rise very little above the earth. Whatever is not God is nothing, and as nothing we ought to reckon it. There is a world of difference between the wisdom of a devout man enlightened by God, and the knowledge of a learned and studious man of letters. Knowledge which streams into the soul from above by the outpouring of God's grace is of a far nobler kind than that which is painfully put together by the efforts of man.

3. You can find a lot of people who long to be contemplatives, but they take no trouble to adopt the practices essential for such a state. It is a great obstacle if we set great store by outward signs and things that affect the senses, and yet hardly bother to bring under stricter control our unruly impulses. By what spirit are we led, I wonder, what are we aiming at, we who would like to be called spiritual men? The trouble we go to, the drudgery we put up with, for the sake of the most ephemeral and unrewarding causes! Yet when it comes to our inner life, how seldom do we give it a thought, how seldom keep our senses completely under control!

4. The sad truth is that after a little time given to meditation we rush straight away and plunge into our outward life, never thinking to weigh on the delicate scales of conscience all that we do. We do not consider where our affections lie, nor grieve for the sinful imperfection of all our actions. *No creature on earth but had lost its true direction*;[1] that was why the great flood came upon them. When our inner longings are full of corruption, the actions to which they give rise must also be corrupted. That is a sign of our lack of inward strength; only from a pure heart comes its natural fruit, a good and holy life.

5. People are concerned to know the greatness of a man's achievements; they are not so interested in assessing the

[1] Gen. 6. 12.

underlying goodness of his life. Is he brave, wealthy, good-looking? Is he a good writer, a good singer, a good worker? Those are the questions they ask. He may be humble, patient, gentle, and live a devout inner life, but you won't get many people to mention any of that. Nature looks at a man from the outside; Grace turns its gaze inward. Nature often makes mistakes; Grace trusts in God, fearing to be deceived.

Chapter 32

ON SELF-DENIAL AND GIVING UP OUR OWN DESIRES

The Beloved: Unless you completely renounce yourself, my son, perfect freedom cannot be yours. What chains bind those who think only of themselves, love but themselves; the greedy, the inquisitive, the gadabouts, those who look for a soft time, and not for Jesus Christ, those who spend their time planning and fashioning things which have no permanence! Yes, everything that has not come from God will pass completely away. Here is a little bit of sound advice: Give up everything, and you shall find everything; renounce desire, and you shall discover peace. Turn that over in your mind; when you have done what it says, you will understand everything.

2. *The Learner:* Lord, that's not going to be child's play; there's more than one day's work there. That short saying sums up the whole of religious perfection.

The Beloved: My son, you must not turn away and immediately lose heart at hearing of the way of perfection. On the contrary, it should be a challenge to you to aim at a higher way of life, or at least to fill your heart with longing for such a life. If only that were so with you; if only you had reached that state where you would no longer be a lover of self, but simply stand ready to do my will and that of the man I have set over you as your Father. You would then be highly pleasing to me, and your whole life would run its course in peace and joy. You have still many things to give up; unless you make them over to me in full, you will not get what you ask for. My advice to you is to buy from me gold refined in the fire, to make you rich;[1] by that I mean heavenly wisdom, that treads underfoot all the base things of earth. Put earthly wisdom behind you, together with all desire to please others or yourself.

3. What I have told you to do is to acquire what in men's eyes appears worthless, instead of what they think valuable and important. True heavenly wisdom seems utterly worthless and insignificant to them; they have almost forgotten it. It holds no high opinion of itself and does not ask for human praise. It is often on the lips of many people—but goes no deeper; their lives are completely at variance with what they extol. Yet it is the precious pearl which is hidden from the eyes of many.

Chapter 33

ON INCONSTANCY OF HEART, AND DIRECTING ALL WE DO TOWARDS GOD

The Beloved: My son, do not trust the affections which now fill your heart; they will soon change into others. As long as you live, you will be subject to changing moods, whether you like it or not. At one moment you will be cheerful, at another depressed; now peaceful, now upset; now full of devotion, now without any at all; now keenly interested, now without heart for anything; now serious, now light-hearted. But your wise man, who has taken thoroughly to heart the lessons of the spiritual life, takes his stand high above all these drifting emotions; he pays no heed to what he may be feeling in himself, does not care from what quarter the wind of inconstant moods may be blowing.

[1] *Cf.* Apoc. 3. 18.

Instead, he directs every aspiration of his heart towards its rightful and desired goal. Thus, by having one single intention in mind, by keeping his gaze fixed on me, without withdrawing it, through all the many and varied happenings of life, he can remain unchanged and unshaken, whatever happens.

2. The more undistracted this intention, this gaze of his remains, the more firm will be his passage through the varying storms that come his way. In many people, however, this undistracted gaze soon grows dim; they soon begin looking at something in their path which takes their fancy. Very rarely will you find anyone completely free from that birth-mark so common in men, self-seeking, I mean. That was the spirit in which the Jews once came to Bethany, to Martha and Mary's; it wasn't just for the sake of Jesus, but to see Lazarus as well. What you must do, then, is to purify your intention, to make it simple and unswerving, so that you may aim it straight at me, passing over all the various things that come between us.

Chapter 34

GOD, ABOVE ALL THINGS AND IN ALL THINGS, IS THE
DELIGHT OF THE LOVING HEART

The Learner: My God, my all, you are here; what more can I wish for, what greater happiness can I desire?

O sweet and delightful word! But sweet only to those who love the Word, not to those who love the world and all that is in the world. My God, my all! To one who understands, that is enough said; to one who loves, it is something to be said over and over again, each time with joy. When you are present, there is joy in everything; when you are not, all things are distasteful. You set the heart at rest, you bring great peace and joy and mirth. You make us think well of all and praise you in all. There is nothing that can please us for long without you; but if it is to be enjoyable and to our taste, your grace must be within it, it needs to be flavoured with the spice of your wisdom.

2. When a man finds delight in you, what is there he will not find delight in? When a man takes no delight in you, what will be able to give him pleasure? But those who are wise in a worldly way, those who have the wisdom of the sensualist, are lacking in your wisdom; the former have nothing but utter emptiness, the latter find death. But those who by scorning worldly ways and chastening their bodily desires follow your own path, they are the really wise men; they have passed from empty folly to truth, from the flesh to the spirit. For such as these, God is their keenest delight: if they *do* find any good in creatures, they make it an additional reason for praising their Maker. But oh! how different, how immeasurably different, is the delight to be found in the Creator and that in things created; how little does eternity resemble time, or uncreated Light the borrowed brightness of creation!

3. O light unending, O light surpassing all that shines in your creation, send down from on high the lightning-stroke of your dazzling brilliance, to pierce and free from darkness the most secret depths of my heart! Seize my spirit and all its powers; give it your purity, your gladness, your brightness, your life, that it may cling to you in an ecstasy of joy. Ah, when will it come, that blissful and longed-for hour, when the joy of your presence shall brim to overflowing the depths of my desire, and you be my all in all? Until you grant me that, my joy cannot be full. Still does the man I was—I grieve to say it—stir to life within me; he is not completely nailed to the cross, not finally and utterly dead. Still do his lusts make violent war against the spirit, making my heart the battle-ground of civil war, so that the kingdom of my soul may not be at peace.

4. Arise and help me, my God, you who govern the might of the sea and calm the turbulent waves! Scatter the nations that delight in war; let that power of yours crush them. Shew them, I beg you, what mighty things you can

do, and let them see the glorious power that lies in your hand; but for you, O Lord my God, I have no hope, no place where I may find shelter.

Chapter 35

WE ARE NEVER SAFE FROM TEMPTATION IN THIS LIFE

The Beloved: You are never safe in this life, my son; as long as you live, you will always need spiritual weapons. It is among your enemies that you spend your days; the attack may come from any quarter. If you fail to use the shield of patience on every side, it will not be long before you get wounded. Besides that, if you neglect to set your heart unwaveringly upon me, with the stark desire of enduring all for my sake, you will be unable to bear the brunt of the assault and will fail to win the palm of victory I award to my blessed ones. You must therefore make your way like a man through all that besets you and strike hard at all that stands in your way; the man who wins through is rewarded with the Bread of Heaven, while the craven is left in the depths of misery.

2. If you try to find rest in this world, how will you ever reach that rest which is life everlasting? It is not long hours of rest you must be prepared for here, but for long hours of patient endurance. True peace must be sought not on earth, but in heaven; not in men, nor in other forms of creation, but in God alone. For the love of God you ought to endure with gladness all that befalls you: toil and sorrow, temptations, afflictions, anxiety, want, weakness, injury and slander, rebuke, humiliation, shame, correction and scorn. All these things are aids to holiness; they test the man who has newly entered the service of Christ, and go to the making of his heavenly crown. For toil soon done I will give a reward that lasts for ever; for fleeting shame, glory without end.

3. Do you imagine you will always have spiritual comfort whenever you want it? That was never the way with my Saints; what *they* had was a world of trouble, trials innumerable, utter desolation. Yet, for all that, they held out patiently in all that befell them, trusting in God and not in themselves; they knew that they did not *count these present sufferings as the measure of that glory which is to be revealed,*[1] the prize they hoped to win. Are you asking to have here and now something that many people have only just managed to obtain after much toil and many a tear? *Wait patiently for the Lord to help you; be brave, and let your heart take comfort.*[2] Do not lose courage, do not retreat; be steadfast in hazarding yourself, body and soul, for the glory of God. The reward I shall give you will surpass all measure, and in all your troubles I shall be at your side.

Chapter 36

AGAINST THE VAIN JUDGEMENTS OF MEN

The Beloved: Let your heart find firm anchorage in the Lord, my son; if your conscience answers your questions by asserting your devotion, your freedom from guilt, do not be afraid how men may judge you. To suffer in such a way is a good and holy thing; to the humble heart, the heart that trusts in God rather than itself, it will be no burden. There are many people who do a great deal of talking; there is no need to pay much attention to what they say. In any case, it's impossible to please everyone. Take St Paul; he made it his business to please everyone in the Lord, and became all things to all men; yet when he was judged by human standards, it meant very little to him.

2. Whatever ability and power he had he used for the spiritual betterment and salvation of others; yet there were

[1] Rom. 8. 18.   [2] Ps. 26. 14.

times when he could not prevent others from passing judgement on him and treating him with scorn. It was for this that he entrusted to God, who knows all things, all that he did; and humbly and patiently defended himself against those who unjustly accused him, those who went to the length of inventing groundless and lying charges against him and those who hurled at him whatever boast they fancied. Sometimes, though, he did return them an answer, if he thought his silence might set those weak in faith stumbling on the road of truth.

3. Who are you, to be afraid of mortal man? Today he is here; tomorrow, his place is empty. Fear God, and then the threats of men will have no terrors for you. What harm can a man do you by his words or his wrongdoing? It is himself he is harming, rather than you; and, whoever he may be, he cannot escape the judgement of God. Keep God before your eyes, and do not get indignant and argue. You may seem for the moment to be losing the battle and suffering undeserved disgrace; but don't let that make you complain, don't, for want of a little patience, dim the lustre of your heavenly crown. Instead, look up to heaven, to me; I have the power to rescue from all shame and wrong, and to give everyone the reward his deeds have deserved.

Chapter 37

SINCERE AND UTTER SELF-RENUNCIATION WINS US FREEDOM OF HEART

The Beloved: Leave yourself behind, my son, and you will find me. Have no choice of your own, no personal preference; you will be the winner every time. The moment you surrender yourself to me, never to take the gift back, a greater store of grace will be added to what you already have.

2. *The Learner:* How often am I to surrender myself,

Lord, and in what matters am I to leave my own preferences behind?

3. *The Beloved:* Always; at every moment, in small things as much as in great. I make no exceptions; it is my wish that in all things you should be stripped naked of self. Otherwise, how are you going to be mine, and I yours, unless you take off every shred of your self-will, whether it shews outwardly or not? The sooner you do this, the better you will feel for it; the more whole-hearted and sincere your surrender, the more you will please me, and the greater will be your gain.

4. There are some who make this surrender, but leave something out; that is because their trust in God is not unreserved, and so they take care to see they are provided for. Again, there are some who at first offer everything, but later on, when temptation has been working on them, they make things their own again, and so advance but little in the ways of holiness. The only way for such as these to reach the real freedom of an unencumbered heart, to be favoured with happy and close friendship with me, is this: they must first make an unconditional surrender, and daily offer themselves to me. Without this, no fruitful union with me can be formed, none endure.

5. I have said this to you a great many times, and now I am saying it once more: Leave yourself behind, surrender yourself, and you will enjoy great inward peace. Give all for all; look for nothing, ask for nothing back. Rest on me, sincerely and without faltering, and you shall have me. Your heart will be free, and no darkness lie heavy upon you. This is what you must strive for, pray for, long for: the power to strip yourself bare of all self-seeking, and naked to follow the naked Jesus; to die to yourself, and be for all eternity alive in me. Then all your foolish fancies will dwindle and die, along with all unreasonable disquiet and needless worry; then, too, will ungovernable fear take leave of you, and love run wild will die.

Chapter 38

ON A GOOD RULE OF LIFE IN OUTWARD MATTERS, AND ON HAVING RECOURSE TO GOD IN DANGER

The Beloved: My son, you should take great care to see that wherever you are and whatever you are doing—outwardly, I mean—you are inwardly free and your own master. Be sure that you have the upper hand of everything, and not the other way about; you must be the master and ruler of all your actions, not their slave or mercenary. You must not be that, but rather one of God's chosen people, a true son of Abraham, sharing the destiny and the freedom of the sons of God. These take their stand above what is now passing, their gaze fixed on what is eternal; they see not only the passing show of life, but heaven too. Such as these are not attracted by the things of time, do not feel bound by them; on the contrary, they take these very things to use in serving God, this being the purpose for which he ordained them and set them in their places, for nothing in the whole of creation has been left without its position in the scheme of things by the great Craftsman who made all that is.

2. Whatever happens, stand firm, and do not judge things you may see or hear by outward appearances or with a worldly eye; in every instance, go like Moses into the Tabernacle and there ask the Lord to advise you. Now and then you will hear God's answer, and return with fresh knowledge of many things, both present and future. It was when Moses was in doubt or had some problem to solve that he had recourse to the Tabernacle; he sought the help to be found in prayer when he found himself beset by danger and the wicked machinations of men. So should you, too, take shelter in the inmost depths of your heart, and there pray earnestly for God's help. It was because they had not first asked counsel of God, so we read, that Joshua and the children of Israel were tricked by the men of Gabaon; the result was that they were too ready to believe those honeyed speeches of theirs, and were taken in by their assumed piety.

Chapter 39

A MAN SHOULD NOT BE
UNREASONABLY ANXIOUS ABOUT HIS AFFAIRS

The Beloved: Always entrust your cause to me, my son; when the proper time comes, I will see that things turn out for the best. Wait for me to arrange matters, and you will realize how much better off you are for it.

2. *The Learner:* Lord, I am glad enough to leave all things in your hands; my own scheming won't get me very far. If only I were not so concerned about future events and could submit myself without any hesitation to your good pleasure.

3. *The Beloved:* My son, a man often goes in eager pursuit of something he wants; when he has got it, he doesn't feel the same about it. Man's affections are unstable, and are apt to drive him from one desirable object to the next, so that even in trivial matters it is well worth renouncing oneself.

4. For a man to make real spiritual progress, he must deny himself; a man who has made this renunciation enjoys great freedom and security. But the Devil, that old enemy of yours, takes no rest from his business of tempting you; day-long, night-long, he is setting his grievous snares, on the chance of tripping the unwary in his hidden nooses. *Watch and pray,* your Lord says, *that you may not enter into temptation.*[1]

Chapter 40

A MAN HAS NO GOODNESS OF HIS OWN,
AND NOTHING TO BOAST OF

The Learner: What is man that you should remember him? What is Adam's breed, that it should claim your care?[2] What has man done, to deserve the gift of your grace? If

[2] Matt. 16. 41.   [1] Ps. 8. 5.

141

you abandon me, Lord, how can I complain? If you don't answer my prayer, what right have I to object? But this is something I can think and say, and it will be true: "Lord, I am nothing, can do nothing; I have no goodness of my own, in nothing do I reach perfection, but have a constant tendency towards nothingness. Unless you help me and work upon my heart I become completely lukewarm and lax."

2. But you, Lord, are always the same and remain so for ever; always good and just and holy, acting always with goodness, justice and holiness, and arranging all things in your wisdom. As for me, I tend to slip back rather than go forward; never do I stay for long in any one state; and I must pass through the seven ages of man, with all their attendant changes. And yet, the moment it pleases you to stretch out your helping hand, I am at once all the better for it; for you alone, without any help from man, can come to my assistance, so strengthening me, that I may no longer direct my gaze this way and that at one thing or another, but turn my heart to you alone, and there find rest.

3. If only I could do without all comfort that comes from man, either to further my devotion or because I needs must seek you, seeing there is no man who can comfort me! I might well then hope for your grace, and rejoice at being given once more your gift of comfort.

4. Every time things go well with me, I thank you, because it all comes from you. In your sight I am but emptiness and nothing, a strengthless, unstable man, so what have I got to be proud of? Why do I long for people to think well of me? Of me, of nothing? Folly can go no further. Such groundless conceit is indeed a canker of the soul and the height of foolishness; it lures a man away from true glory and strips him bare of heavenly grace. So long as a man is foolishly pleased with himself, to you he is only displeasing; so long as he covets the good opinion of men, he is depriving himself of true virtue.

5. The real way to take pride and be filled with holy joy is to take pride not in oneself but in you, to rejoice in your name, not in one's own strength, and to find no pleasure in

anything created except for your sake. May your name be praised, not mine; your works commended, not mine; may your holy name be blessed, but let me have no share in the praises of men. You are my pride and glory, the joy of my heart. In you I will take pride and rejoice the livelong day; in myself I will take no pride, except perhaps in my own weaknesses.

6. Let the Jews seek the kind of glory that men give one another; the glory I shall seek is that which is given by God alone. All human glory, all this world's honours, all high positions on earth, look meaningless and silly when set beside your everlasting glory. O blessed Trinity, my God, my truth, my mercy, to you alone belong praise, honour, power and glory, through endless ages and ages.

Chapter 41

ON DESPISING THIS WORLD'S HONOURS

The Beloved: Don't take it to heart, son, if you see others winning honours and promotion, and yourself being looked down upon and treated like dirt. Lift up your heart to heaven, to me, and being slighted by men on earth won't make you sad any more.

2. *The Learner:* Lord, we live in a world of blindness and are easily led away by foolish notions. Passing my life in frank review, I see that no creature has ever done me harm, so that I have no right to have any grievance against you; but seeing how often and how grievously I have sinned against you, it is but right that every creature should be up in arms against me. All I deserve, then, and rightly so, is shame and scorn, but you, praise, honour and glory. Unless I make myself ready and willing to be slighted and left to myself by every creature, to be regarded as a complete nonentity, I cannot win inward peace and stability, cannot be enlightened in spirit and fully united to you.

Chapter 42

OUR PEACE OF MIND MUST NOT DEPEND UPON MEN

The Beloved: If you let your peace of mind depend on any particular person, my son, because you enjoy his affection and companionship, you will live an unsettled life and get entangled in your own feelings; but if you have recourse to the Truth that lives and remains for ever, your friend will not make you sad even though he leaves you or dies. The love you have for your friend ought to rest on me; it is for my sake that they must be loved, those whose goodness appeals to you, those most dear to you in this life. Without me, no friendship will hold fast or endure; in every genuine and sincere love I am the connecting link. You ought to be so mortified in the affection you have for those you love that, as far as you are concerned, you could wish to do without human companionship altogether. The further a man goes from any comfort upon earth, the nearer he draws to God; the deeper he goes down within himself, the lower he sinks in his own estimation, so much the higher does he climb in his ascent towards God.

2. A man who attributes any goodness to himself puts up a barrier against the coming of God's grace, because it is always a humble heart that the grace of the Holy Ghost looks for. If only you would reduce your self-seeking to nothing, and empty your heart of love for anything created, my grace would be bound to flood your heart in fathomless streams. So long as you gaze at things created, you lose sight of him who created them. It is for the sake of that Creator that you must learn to overcome yourself in everything; you will then be enabled to come to the knowledge of God. If the love and interest you have for anything, no matter how trivial, is lacking in restraint, it is holding you back from attaining your highest goal, and doing you harm.

Chapter 43

A CONDEMNATION OF
USELESS AND WORLDLY LEARNING

The Beloved: My son, you must not let yourself be impressed by the fine and clever things you hear men say; *it is power that builds up the kingdom of God, not words.*[1] Pay heed to my words, which bring fire to the heart and light to the mind, piercing the heart with sorrow for sin and filling it with comfort in many ways. Never read anything to enable you to appear better-educated or wiser than your fellows. What you ought to study is the way to kill off your worst faults; that will do you far more good than knowing all about a number of vexatious problems.

2. You may have done a lot of reading, and found out a great deal about a variety of subjects, but the basic fact you must always come back to is this: that I am he who teaches men whatever they know; to those of child-like simplicity I give a clearer understanding than any man can teach. When I speak to a man, he soon becomes wise and goes far along the paths of the spirit. It will go ill with those who are always after odd fragments of worldly information, and yet never give a thought to the way they ought to be serving me. The time will come when Christ shall appear, he who is the Teacher of all teachers and Lord of the Angels; he will hear each of you say his lesson, that is, examine his conscience. That will be the time for Jerusalem to be searched with lamps; things hidden in darkness will be brought to light, and wrangling tongues keep quiet.

3. I am he who in a moment can so lift up the mind of a humble man that he has a firmer grasp of the ways of eternal truth than the man who has spent ten years studying the subject at a University. I teach without clamour of words, without the clash of opinions, without place-seeking, without obstinate wrangling. And this is the lesson I teach: to look down on the things of earth, to grow weary of this

[1] 1 Cor. 4. 20.

present life, to seek and find pleasure in what is eternal, to avoid honours, to bear with injuries, to trust me unreservedly, to desire nothing apart from me; above all, to love me with passionate devotion.

4. There was once a man who by his deep love for me learned the things of God, and people were filled with wonder at what he spoke of; he had done better for himself by giving up everything than he would have done by studying intricate arguments. To some I give messages meant for all men, to others I speak for their own sake alone. There are some who are glad to see me in signs and symbols, while for others I throw a full flood of light on the mysteries I disclose to them. Books have only one meaning, but one man will get more out of them than another; it is I who in them teach men the truth, search their hearts, understand their thoughts, help on their actions, giving each of them whatever share of my gifts I reckon they deserve.

Chapter 44

ON NOT BEING CONCERNED WITH OUTWARD THINGS

The Beloved: There are a good many things, my son, about which you should be ignorant. You ought to think of yourself as being dead, though still on earth; the whole world ought to seem to you as dead as if it were nailed to a cross. There are a lot of things it is as well to turn a deaf ear to; far better to think of things that keep your mind at peace. It is better to look the other way when you see something not to your liking, better to leave everyone to think as he pleases than to feel bound to begin a heated argument. If you are pleasing in the sight of God and are concerned only with his view of the matter in question, you won't mind it so much when you are worsted by others.

2. *The Learner:* Lord, what a state things have got into these days! You know how miserable we get over some

worldly loss, and how we work hard and rush around to gain some little advantage; as for the damage done to our spiritual life, we quickly forget about it and even later on can scarcely call it to mind. We give all our attention to things that do us little good, or none at all; things that are vitally necessary we don't bother about and just give them the go-by. Yes, all that goes to make man drives him to meddle with outward things, and if he doesn't soon recover his senses, he is only too glad to wallow in material interests and pleasures.

Chapter 45

WE SHOULD NOT BELIEVE EVERYONE; HOW EASY IT IS FOR WORDS TO SLIP OUT

The Learner: Help me in my trouble, Lord; there is no sure help to be found in man.[1] How often have I put my trust in someone, and then found him disloyal! Again, how often have I found loyalty where I should least have thought to find it! So it's no good putting our trust in men; it is you alone, my God, that a good man may trust without fear of betrayal. May you be blessed, O Lord my God, in all that befalls us. A weak and shiftless lot we are, Lord, easily taken in, easily changing from one thing to another.

2. There isn't anyone able to keep so careful and all-embracing a watch on himself as not to find himself, now and then, mistaken or at fault; it isn't so easy for a man to slip if he puts his trust in you, Lord, and seeks you in singleness of heart. And if he meets with some trouble or other, no matter how he has got himself mixed up in it, you will quickly get him out of it and comfort him; you never abandon those who trust you to the end. Rarely will you find a friend so faithful as to stick by his friend in all his troubles. You, Lord, are the only friend who is ever

[1] *Cf.* Ps. 59. 13.

faithful, whatever happens; no one else can come anywhere near you for that.

3. There was once a holy soul—St Agatha—who said: "My mind has Christ for its foundation and support"; how wise she was! If only I could make those words mine, it would not be so easy for me to be troubled by fear of this man or that; the sting of their words would leave me unhurt. No one can foresee everything that's going to happen or take precautions against future disasters. We are often hurt by things we have seen coming at us; bolts from the blue can hardly do otherwise than leave us prostrate. But why haven't I made better plans against the future—I shall suffer for it—and why have I been so ready to trust others? We are only men, after all, nothing but weak men, though a lot of people think and talk about us as though we were angels. Whom can I trust, Lord? No one but you; you are the Truth, and we cannot deceive you, nor you us. *Man's faith is false*;[1] he is weak, shiftless, fallible, especially when he is speaking; something may sound all right when he says it, but we should not be too ready to believe it there and then.

4. You wisely gave us due warning about being on guard against men: *a man's own household are his enemies*;[2] you warned us not to believe if anyone told us, *See, he is here* or *See, he is there*.[3] That is something I have learned to my cost; I hope it will make me more careful in future and not so silly. "Don't tell a soul," someone says; "don't tell a soul; keep this under your hat." And while I keep quiet and think I am sharing a secret, the fellow himself can't hold his tongue about what he asked me to keep secret, but loses no time in betraying both himself and me, and then off he goes. Lord, keep me from that kind of gossip, from people who can't bridle their tongue; don't let me fall into their hands, and never let me do that kind of thing myself. Make whatever I say be true and sound; let my talk never come near what is sly and malicious. If I hate that kind of thing in others, I must make quite certain I don't do it myself.

[1] Ps. 115. 2. [2] Matt. 10. 36 [3] Matt. 24. 23.

5. It is a very good thing, one that brings you peace, not to talk about other people, not to be taken in by all you hear and not to seize the first chance of spreading a story further. There should not be many in whom we confide unreservedly, but we ought always to seek you, Lord, you who can see into our hearts. It is not for us to veer about in every wind of conversation, but to hope that all our life, both inward and outward, may be lived as best pleases your will. If we want to keep hold of heavenly grace, the safest thing is to avoid appearing in public and not to hanker after the kind of things that win admiration in the outside world; but instead, to apply ourselves with the utmost zeal to whatever makes us change our life for the better and promotes spiritual fervour. A lot of people have come to grief through having their virtues discovered and applauded when they were scarcely in bud. Grace is most beneficial, no doubt of it, when stored in silence during this uncertain life, a life which is nothing but temptation and warfare.

Chapter 46

ON PUTTING OUR TRUST IN GOD WHEN OTHERS MAKE STINGING REMARKS

The Beloved: Stand your ground, son, and trust in me. What are words, after all? Only words. They hurtle through the air, but they can't as much as scratch a stone. If you have done wrong, think how willingly you would turn over a new leaf; if your conscience is clear, make up your mind to endure this for God's sake. It's not so much to put up with, a few unpleasant remarks now and then, if you're not yet able to bear a sound thrashing. If you take such little things so much to heart, it's because you're still a worldly man and mind what people say much more than you should. You are anxious not to be looked down on, so

149

you dislike being rebuked for your faults, and try to hide behind a screen of excuses.

2. Take a better look at yourself, and you will admit that worldly ideas are still very much alive in you, that you still have a senseless desire to please people. When you shrink from being put in your place and reprimanded for your faults, it is quite clear that you are not really humble, not really dead to the world; nor does the world stand crucified to you. Only listen to the words I speak, and you will not mind, even if men speak ten thousand words against you. Put it this way; suppose people made up the most malicious accusations against you they could think of. What harm could they all do you if you just let them go by you, not taking the smallest bit of notice? Do you think they could as much as remove a single hair from your head?

3. A man who lets his heart wander where it likes, a man whose gaze is not fixed on God, is easily put out by a word of rebuke; but the man who trusts in me and has no wish to stand by his own judgement will dread no man. That is because I am the one who judges, who knows all secrets; I see in what way a thing has been done; I know both him who does wrong to another and him who suffers that wrong. It is from me that he draws the power to act so; it is by my permission that it happens in that way, that the thoughts of many hearts may be made manifest. I will judge the guilty and the innocent, but first I wish to try them in my own secret court of justice.

4. What men say in evidence is often untrue; my verdict is a true one, which shall stand and not be set aside. It is hidden for the most part, though some may catch a glimpse of certain clauses in it. It never makes a mistake, never can, though unthinking people may imagine it seems unfair. So, when you need a decision on some disputed question, have recourse to me and do not let your personal views have any weight with you. A man of good life will not be disquieted, whatever comes to him from the hand of God. Even though a false charge is laid at his door, it will not worry him very much. On the other, if others duly acquit him, he will not

make it an occasion for senseless rejoicing. That is because he is well aware that is it I who search men's hearts and inner motives; my verdict does not go by the face of things, by the way things look to men. From my point of view, something is often to be condemned, though as men see it it earns their approval.

5. *The Learner:* Lord God, you who as a judge are just, patient and strong, you who know the frailty and crookedness of men, I ask you to be my strength, that I may put complete trust in you; my conscience by itself is not enough. You know what I do not; that should have made me humble myself whenever I was reprimanded, made me meekly bear the reproof. Be merciful; forgive me for all the times I have failed to act in that way; give me grace once more to endure things for longer than I have. The flood of your mercy will better avail me if I would be pardoned, than my protestation of innocence will be echoed by my inmost conscience. I may not be conscious of any fault, but that is no reason for complacency; if you withhold your mercy, *what man is there living that can stand guiltless in your presence?*[1]

Chapter 47

ALL TROUBLES MUST BE BORNE
FOR THE SAKE OF ETERNAL LIFE

The Beloved: My son, do not let the hard work you have taken on for my sake crush you; do not let any trouble make you lose heart completely. In all that happens, let my promise be your strength and consolation. The reward I have in store for you is both boundless and measureless. The time you are working here will not be long; you will not always have sorrows pressing upon you. Wait but a little while, and you will see all your miseries vanish in a trice. The time is coming when all your toil and trouble will be

[1] Ps. 142. 2.

no more; anything that passes with the passing of time cannot but be short-lived, cannot but matter little.

2. Go on with what you are doing; work faithfully in my vineyard; the reward you will have is myself. Go on writing, reading, singing, sighing, keeping silence, bearing your troubles like a man; it is well worth fighting all your present battles, and even greater ones, to gain eternal life. Peace will come at a time known only to the Lord; there will not be day and night as we know them now, but light that never wanes, brightness that has no bounds, peace never to be broken, rest that shall never be disturbed. You will not say then, *Who is to set me free from a nature thus doomed to death?*[1] neither will you cry, *Unhappy I, that the days of my sojourn have been prolonged!*[2] for death will be cast headlong, and salvation no more be in danger; no anguish then to torment you, but only blessed joy, and the sweet and lovely companionship of heaven.

3. If only you had seen the crowns of unfailing glory worn by the Saints in heaven, seen how greatly they now rejoice there, though once the world scoffed at them and thought them hardly fit to live; you would certainly make yourself the lowest of the low and long to be at everyone's beck and call rather than lord it over a single person. You would not want to have a good time in this world, but be glad to endure trouble for God's sake; as for being thought nothing of by men, that would seem to you the greatest of advantages.

4. If you were really keen to get to heaven, if the thought of it went right home to your inmost heart, how would you have the affrontery to voice a single grievance? Surely, with eternal life as the prize, you ought to put up with all kinds of hardship. It's not a small matter, you know, this losing or gaining the kingdom of God. So look up to heaven; that is where I am, and with me all my Saints who in this life had a hard struggle of it; here at this very moment they are rejoicing, at this very moment comforted, safe and at rest; and here in the kingdom of my Father they will stay in my company for time without end.

[1] Rom. 7. 24. [2] Ps. 119. 5 according to the Vulgate.

AN EXILE'S PRAYER

Chapter 48

ON THE DAY OF ETERNITY
AND THE TROUBLES OF THIS LIFE

The Learner: How happy are those who dwell for ever in the city that is above! How bright is the day of eternity! It is a day upon which night casts no shadow, but one for ever lit by the very Truth; a day for ever happy, for ever safe, a day that never changes into the contrary. Oh, how I wish that day had already dawned, and all these things of time come to an end! For the Saints, that day is already shining, bright with a radiance that goes on and on; for us who are still making our earthly pilgrimage, it shines only from a distance; we can see its reflection, so to speak, only in a looking-glass.

2. Those who are townsmen of the heavenly city know how joyful the day is there; we, the outcast children of Eve, know how bitter and wearisome the day can be on earth. Yes, the days of time are few and evil indeed, full of sorrow and trouble. Here man is befouled by many sins, enmeshed in many passions, brushed close by many fears. He is tormented by many cares, dragged this way and that by many strange sights, entangled in many kinds of folly. Many an error surrounds him, many a hard task leaves him exhausted; he is burdened with temptations, enfeebled by pleasures, racked with want.

3. Oh, when will these evils come to an end? When shall I be freed from the wretched slavery of sin? Lord, when shall I think only of you, find in you my full measure of gladness? When shall I be really free, with nothing to hinder me, nothing to drag me down in mind or body? When will there be lasting peace, peace for ever safe and never to be disturbed, peace both within and without, peace that in every way stands unchanged? Good Jesus, when shall I stand in your sight and see you? When shall I gaze upon the glory of your kingdom? When will you be all in all to me? Oh, when shall I be in that kingdom of yours which you have

153

made ready from all time for those you love? Here I have been left behind in enemy territory, a poor outcast in a land where every day there is fighting, every day disasters most dire.

4. Comfort me in this my exile; assuage my grief; it is to you that I sigh with all my longing. Whatever this world can offer me by way of comfort is nothing but a burden to me; I long for the bliss of your close company, but I am unable to reach so far. I yearn to hold fast to heavenly things, but I am weighed down by the things of the time, by passions far from dead. With my mind I long to rise superior to all these things, but my body compels me to be their unwilling slave. Thus it comes about that I, poor piece of humanity, am the theatre of civil war, a burden to myself, with the spirit trying to soar aloft, and the body endeavouring to stay below.

5. What I go through inwardly, when my mind is groping its way towards the things of heaven, and, during my very prayer, a crowd of worldly thoughts comes rushing into my head! Do not go far away from me, my God, do not turn away in anger from this servant of yours. Dazzle them with the stroke of your lightning, and scatter them; shoot forth your arrows, and so put to rout all the drifting thoughts sent by my enemy. Gather my senses together and fix them on yourself; make me forget all that is in the world; give me the power to hurl back and to scorn all mental pictures of evil deeds. Come to my help, O everlasting Truth, so that no empty folly may sway my heart. O heavenly sweetness, come to me, and all that is foul will flee at sight of you. Forgive me, also, and in your mercy grant me pardon for all the times I think of anything besides you in time of prayer; because, to confess the truth, I am usually in a state of great distraction. Often enough I am not where my body is, whether standing or sitting, but wherever my thoughts carry me to. Wherever my thoughts are, there am I; and my thoughts are usually with the things I love. What comes most readily to mind is something naturally pleasant or found by experience to be agreeable.

6. It was this that made you, the very Truth, say plainly: *Where your treasure-house is, there your heart is too.*[1] If I love heaven, I readily think of heavenly things; if I love the world, I share the world's gladness when it rejoices, and am sad when it is thwarted. If I love the body, I often picture to myself bodily delights; if I love the spirit, I love thinking about spiritual matters. Whatever it is that I like best, those are the things I love talking and hearing about; and I bring home mental pictures of them with me from the world outside. But happy is the man who for your sake, Lord, has, so to speak, given all things created notice to quit; the man who gets tough with nature and crucifies the lusts of his body with the burning desires of his spirit. Such a man has put his conscience at rest and can offer you unblemished prayer; by closing the door on earthly interests, both in his life and in his heart, he is worthy to mingle with the choirs of angels.

Chapter 49

ON LONGING FOR ETERNAL LIFE, AND THE JOYS PROMISED TO THOSE WHO FIGHT TO GAIN THAT LIFE

The Beloved: My son, when you feel the desire for everlasting bliss streaming into you from on high; when you thirst to leave that body in which you are now, as it were, camping for a time, so as to be able to gaze on my glory, that glory on which there falls no shadow of change: open your heart wide, and welcome this holy inspiration with all the longing you have. Thank me again and again for my divine bounty in dealing thus with you so generously, visiting you in my mercy, stirring you with the fire of my love, uplifting you with my strength, and so preventing you from falling down again into those worldly ways to which you gravitate so naturally. You must not take this favour

[1] Matt. 6. 21.

to be the result of your own meditations, your own exertions; it is yours only because the grace of heaven has come down to help you, because God has looked on you in love. Its purpose is to make you advance in holiness, to make you more deeply humble, better prepared for conflicts yet to come; it is to make you cling close to me with all the love of your heart, to make you long to serve me with willing devotion.

2. There are often fires burning, my son, but not a flame shoots upward without smoke beside it. That is the way with a lot of people who are afire for heavenly things; the flame is there well enough, but they are not free from the temptation of bodily desire. Thus it is that, for all the longing they put into their prayers, they do not offer them solely for the honour of God. That is often the way with your own desire, though you may have persuaded yourself your prayers were going to be perfectly sincere; but no prayer can be called perfect or free from blemish when there is some tincture of self-interest in it.

3. Do not ask me for things to make life pleasant and comfortable for you; ask for what is acceptable to me, for whatever brings me honour. If you look on things in the way you should, you ought to prefer my way of ordering things, and keep to it, rather than ask for the fulfilment of your own desires or for the keeping of something you have desired before. I know what your desires are; I have heard what you so often sigh for. You would like to be at this moment amid the freedom and the glory of the children of God, enjoying your eternal home and the abounding happiness of the heavenly country; but the time for that has not yet come. You are still, for the moment, in another kind of time—wartime it is, a time of toil and trial. You long to be filled with the supreme good, but that bliss is not to be arrived at now. I am speaking of myself; wait for me, the Lord says, until the coming of the kingdom of God.

4. There is still a time of trial for you on earth; you must be tested in many ways. Sometimes you will be given consolation, but it will not be granted you in full abundance;

so take heart and be strong, whether doing or enduring what goes against nature. You have to clothe yourself in a new kind of manhood, change into another kind of person. Often you will have to do what you dislike, and forgo doing what you would like to do. Other people's interests will prosper, your own make no headway; others will be listened to when they speak, but people will take no notice of anything you say. Others will ask for things, and get them; when you ask, your request will be in vain.

5. People will say a lot of nice things about others; no one will say a word about you. Others will be given this or that position of trust; you will be reckoned good for nothing at all. Naturally, this kind of thing will make you sad now and then, but if you bear it all without saying a word, you have taken a great step forward. These are the ways—these and many others like them—by which a faithful servant of the Lord is usually tested, to see how he can renounce himself and break his own will in everything. There is hardly anything in which you need so much to die to yourself as to see and suffer things that are opposed to your own wishes. This is especially so when things are ordered to be done which to your mind are quite out of keeping and completely useless. Being under obedience to another, as you are, you dare not stand up to one higher in authority, and so you think it hard to have to live your life at another's beck and call and disregard your own feelings.

6. But think, my son, of the reward these hardships are going to win you; think how soon they will end, how great is the prize you will be given. Then you will not feel the weight of them; instead, they will comfort you and be a strong support to your will to endure. In return for the free surrender of what little choice you have in earthly things, in heaven you shall always have your own way. Yes, there you shall find all you have ever wanted, all you could ever desire. There every kind of delight will be yours to have, and you will never be afraid of losing it. There will your will and my will be ever as one, and you will desire nothing I do not desire, nothing for yourself alone. There shall be no one to

157

withstand you there, no one to complain, no one to hinder or thwart you; but all you have ever desired will be there together, giving joy to your powers of love and filling them to the very brim. There, for the shame you have suffered, I will give you glory; in place of the garb of mourning, a robe of honour; instead of the lowest place, a seat in my kingdom for ever. There your obedience shall be rewarded in the sight of all; your hard penance shall be turned to joy, and your lowly subjection receive a crown of glory.

7. During this present life, then, behave humbly towards all men, and do not mind who says this or who orders that, but take great care that whenever anyone asks you for something or makes some suggestion, whether he be your superior, your equal, or one below you, take it all in good part and with unfeigned willingness try to do what they say. Let other men have their ambitions in one direction or another, one man priding himself on his ability in one field, another in something different, and getting praised for it any number of times; you must take pleasure in none of these things, but only in being slighted and in my good pleasure and honour alone. This is what you must desire: that in you, whether by your life or by your death, God may always be glorified.

Chapter 50

HOW A MAN OUGHT TO PUT HIMSELF IN GOD'S HANDS IN TIME OF TROUBLE

The Learner: Lord God, holy Father, may you be blessed both now and for ever; whatever happens comes about because you wish it so; and what you do is good. I am your servant; let me rejoice not in myself or in any other, but in you, because you alone are my real happiness; you are my hope and my crown, Lord, my joy and my honour. What does this servant of yours possess that he has not received from you, and that through no merit of his own? Everything is yours, both what you have given and what you have made. *Ever since youth, misery and mortal sickness have been my lot;*[1] often enough I am so sad at heart that my eyes fill with tears, and sometimes my soul is in turmoil because of the strong feelings that oppress it.

2. I long for the joy of your peace, praying hard for the peace enjoyed by your children who are allowed by you to roam the shining pastures of your consolation. If you give me this peace, if you flood my heart with holy joy, my soul will burst into joyful song and devote itself to praising you; but if you withdraw from me, as you do so often, I shall be unable to run on the road of your commandments. Instead, on bended knees I shall beat my breast, because my life is no longer what it was yesterday and the day before, when your lantern gleamed above my head, and I found in the shelter of your wings a refuge from the temptations that assailed me.

3. Father of all justice, you who are ever to be praised, the hour has come for the testing of this servant of yours. Father to whom all love is due, it is right that your servant should suffer something on this occasion for your sake. Father to whom we owe unceasing worship, the time has come which you foresaw from all eternity would meet me, the time for your servant to fall low for a while in the eyes of the world, though in your sight his inner life remains ever as it was. For a short time he must be scoffed at, humiliated and brought low in the eyes of men, tormented by the vehemence of his feelings and by weakness, that with you he may rise again in the dawn of a new day, and in heaven be clothed with glory. Holy Father, that is the way you have decreed it should happen, the way you have willed it; what has happened has happened by your command.

4. That is the way you shew favour to any friend of yours: you let him suffer and meet with trouble in this world, for love of you; the number of times this shall happen, and the instrument of his affliction, are determined by your per-

[1] Ps. 87. 16.

mission, for nothing on earth takes place that has not been planned by you, foreseen by you; nothing happens by chance. *It was in mercy you did chasten me, schooling me to your obedience*;[1] I will renounce all elation of heart, all presumption. It is good for me to have known disgrace; let it make me seek you, rather than men, to bring me comfort. Another lesson I have learned from this experience, that of standing in dread of your unsearchable judgement; because you afflict the good along with the wicked, yet not without being fair and just in your judgement.

5. Thank you for not sparing my evildoing, but for chastising me instead with the lash of bitter grief, afflicting me with sorrows and sending me troubles both inward and outward. There is nothing can comfort me, of everything beneath the heavens, but you alone, my Lord and my God; you are the heavenly healer, the Lord of life and death, *who brings men to the grave and back from the grave*;[2] your tender care is above me; your very rod teaches me a lesson.

6. See, my beloved Father, I am in your hands; I bend low to take the blows of your chastening rod. Strike me where you will, across the back, across the neck, and make me bring my crooked ways in line with your will. Make a loving and humble pupil of me, as you have so often made others, one who will take a step only at a sign from you. To you, Lord, I offer for your correction both myself and all that is mine; it is better to be punished here than in the world to come. You know all that is, and every single part of that all; for you no one's conscience has any secrets. You know the future before it comes along; and you have no need of anyone to tell you what is happening on earth. You know what I need if I am to make any progress, know how efficient much trouble can be in scrubbing away the rust of my sins. Make me long to do what pleases you best, and do not scorn my sinful life, that no one knows better or more clearly than you alone.

7. Lord, grant that I may know what I ought to know, love what I ought to love, praise what best pleases you,

[1] Ps. 118. 71.   [2] Tobias 13. 2.

value what you deem precious, condemn whatever in your eyes seems filthy. Let me not judge things by outward appearances or form my opinions on the hearsay of those who know but little; give me that true judgement which can form a correct opinion on matters both of the world we see and that other world of the spirit; and let me above all else ever seek what best pleases your will.

8. Men's senses often lead them astray when it comes to deciding any matter; there are others led astray, too, by loving only what they can see, I mean the lovers of this world. What does a man gain from being held in high repute by someone else? When one man praises another, it is a case of one hypocrite deceiving his fellow hypocrite, the blind cheating the blind, the weak the weak; and so meaningless the praise is, it's really more of a disgrace to its recipient than anything else. "What every man is in your sight, Lord, that is what he is, and nothing more"; it was the humble St Francis who said that.

Chapter 51

WE SHOULD BUSY OURSELVES WITH HUMBLE TASKS
WHEN WE FAIL TO REACH HIGHER KINDS OF
OCCUPATION

The Beloved: My son, you cannot always be in a state of burning desire for holiness, cannot always remain in the higher reaches of contemplation. You have to come down to earth now and then—your fallen nature demands it—and shoulder the load of this life of constant decay, however much you dislike it and are weary of it. So long as you wear that mortal body of yours, you will feel weary and heavy at heart. While you are yet in the body, then, you ought often to complain of the burden that the body is to you, preventing you from giving all your time to the things of the spirit and to divine contemplation.

THE IMITATION OF CHRIST

2. At such times it is as well for you to take to humble, outward occupations, and to restore your spiritual strength by performing various good deeds. You should also wait with unwavering trust for me to come and visit you from on high, and patiently bear your exile and unsatisfied spiritual thirst until I visit you once more and free you from all that torments you. Then I will make you forget your troubles and you shall enjoy inward peace. I will spread out before you the meadows of Holy Scripture, so that, your heart no more a prisoner, you may begin to run along the road of my commandments. Then you will say, *I do not count these present sufferings as the measure of that glory which is to be revealed in us.*[1]

Chapter 52

A MAN OUGHT TO THINK HE DESERVES NOT CONSOLATION BUT PUNISHMENT

The Learner: Lord, I am unworthy of your comfort, and indeed of any spiritual approach of yours. When you leave me poor and forsaken, I am getting no more than my due. If I could shed as many tears as there are drops in the sea, I should still be unworthy of consolation. No, all I deserve is whipping and punishment, for many is the time I have offended you—gravely, too—and many the evil deeds I have done. So, looking at things as they really are, I do not deserve the least bit of comfort. But you are the God of mercy, the God of pity; it is not your will that what you have made should perish. You would shew the riches of your lovingkindness, pouring them into empty vessels which await your mercy; and therefore you stoop from heaven to console this servant of yours beyond anything he could have deserved, and in a way surpassing human ken; because your consolation is a very different thing from the empty mouthings of men.

[1] Rom. 8. 18.

2. What have I done, Lord, for you to bring me any comfort from heaven? I have never done any good, as far as I know, but have always been prone to sin and slow to amend. That is the truth, and I cannot deny it; if I said anything else, you would confront me, and there would be no one to defend me. What have I deserved for my sins but hell and everlasting fire? All I deserve, frankly speaking, is to be scoffed at and scorned; I am not good enough to be counted among your devoted servants. This is going to make painful hearing for me, but for truth's sake I will accuse myself of my sins, in the hope that I may deserve the more readily to win your merciful forgiveness.

3. Yes, I am guilty, one mass of shame; what am I to say? Not a word will come; all I can say is, "I have sinned, Lord, I have sinned; have mercy on me and pardon me". *For a little leave me to myself, to find some comfort in my misery. Soon I must go to a land whence there is no returning, a land of darkness, death's shadow over it.*[1] Why are you so insistent in asking a poor, guilty sinner to repent and humble himself for the wrong he has done? It is because from real repentance and humbleness of heart is born the hope of pardon; the conscience that was troubled is restored to God's favour, the grace that has been lost is returned, and man is shielded from the wrath to come. God and the penitent soul run to meet each other with a holy kiss.

4. Humble repentance for sin is a welcome sacrifice to you, Lord; it is far more fragrant in your sight than the smoke of burned incense. It is also the sweet ointment which you once desired to have poured over your feet; for you have never despised a contrite and humble heart. It is there that we can find a place of shelter from the face of our raging enemy; it is there that whatever has somehow got broken is mended, whatever has been soiled washed clean again.

[1] Job 10. 20, 21.

Chapter 53

GOD'S GRACE AND WORLDLY WISDOM DO NOT MIX

The Beloved: My grace, son, is something precious; it will not stand being mixed up with worldly interests and earthly comforts; so, if you hope to have it poured into your soul, you must remove everything which might clog its path. Search out for yourself some out-of-the-way spot, and make it your delight to live there alone by yourself. Don't go looking for neighbours to pass the time of day with, but talk to God in prayerful entreaty, if you want to remain sorry for your sins and keep your conscience clean. Count the whole world as nothing; put your waiting on God before all outward things, because you will not be able to attend to me and at the same time take pleasure in the passing things of time. Friends and acquaintances you should keep at a distance, and have your heart always empty of this world's consolations. That is what St Peter means when he entreats Christ's faithful servants to keep themselves as *strangers and pilgrims*[1] in this world.

2. When a man is about to meet death, what confidence it will give him if he has no love for anything created to hold him back in this world! But your weakly soul cannot yet bear to have his heart thus detached from all things; your sensualist cannot grasp the freedom of the man whose life is that of the spirit. All the same, if anyone really wants to live a spiritual life, he must give up all, the friends at his side no less than the distant places he might have been to; and there is no one he must beware of more than himself. Once you have gained complete mastery of yourself, it will be all the easier to bring everything else under your control. There can be no greater victory than to triumph over oneself. The man who has such command of himself that his sensual feelings obey his reason and his reason in everything obeys me is indeed master of himself and ruler of the world.

[1] 1 Peter 2. 11.

3. If it is your earnest desire to scale this peak of spirituality, you must start off like a man by laying the axe to the roots; hack out and destroy that lurking, uncontrolled leaning towards yourself and towards any personal and material gain. It is this vice of uncontrolled self-love that underlies nearly all else in a man that must be pulled up by the roots; once this particular fault has been mastered and brought under, he will at once be conscious of great peace and inward quiet. There are not many, though, who endeavour to die completely to themselves, to soar right above their own nature; the result is that most people remain caught in the nets of their own being, unable to rise above themselves in spirit. The man who desires to walk untrammelled in my company must mortify all his warped and ill-regulated desires, and not attach his longings to any creature, any personal object of love.

Chapter 54

ON THE OPPOSITION BETWEEN
THE WORKINGS OF NATURE AND GRACE

The Beloved: My son, you must carefully notice the ways in which nature moves, and grace; these two ways are completely opposed, but so fine and hidden as hardly to be told apart, except by a spiritual man gifted with inward light. All men desire what is good, and make out there is some good in whatever they do or say; that is why many people are taken in by a kind of good that is so only in appearance.

2. Nature is crafty, many are those she betrays, ensnaring and deceiving them, ever having her own ends in view; Grace makes her way unaffectedly, turning aside from anything that looks evil. She tries no trickery, but does everything simply for the sake of God, in whom she rests, making him the end of whatever she does.

3. Nature is loth to be put to death, to be repressed or overcome, to be obedient or to be a willing subject; Grace seeks to mortify herself, withstands the sensual feelings, seeks to be under authority, desires to be overcome, and has no wish to enjoy personal freedom; she loves being kept under discipline, and has no desire to lord it over anyone else. All she wants is always to live, to remain and to exist under God's direction, and for his sake she is ready to submit humbly to every member of the human race.

4. Nature works to advance her own interests, waiting to see how much gain will be coming to her from others. Grace, on the other hand, does not consider what may be of profit or advantage to herself, but what may benefit many.

5. Nature is glad to receive honour and respect; Grace faithfully ascribes all honour and glory to God.

6. Nature is afraid of disgrace and scorn; Grace is glad to suffer shame for the name of Jesus.

7. Nature loves taking it easy, loves giving the body rest; Grace cannot be unoccupied, but is glad to take up some work.

8. Nature collects rare and beautiful things and disdains what is coarse and cheap; Grace is pleased with simple, humble things, does not look askance at what is rough or jib at dressing in old rags.

9. Nature has her eye on worldly matters, is cheered by material gain and grieved by its loss, and is stung to anger by the least unkind remark; but Grace is concerned with what is eternal, is not attached to the things of time. The loss of her goods does not worry her, nor is she embittered by the harsh comments of others, because she has placed her treasure and her joy in heaven, where nothing is ever lost.

10. Nature is greedy; she would much rather receive than give, and holds on to her property with possessive love; Grace is kind and unselfish, believes in sharing, is quite happy with little, and reckons that giving presents makes one happier than receiving them.

11. Nature has a tendency towards creatures, towards a man's own body, as well as to foolish pastimes and unnecessary gadding about; Grace draws a man towards God and holy living. She renounces creatures, shuns the world, hates the lusts of the flesh, cuts down occasions for wandering abroad, and blushes to appear in public.

12. Nature is glad of any outward comfort that pleases the senses; Grace seeks comfort in God alone, and above all that the eye can see takes pleasure in him who is the sovereign good.

13. Everything Nature does is for her own profit and advantage; she can never do any job for nothing, but hopes to have her services repaid in equal measure or by something extra, or else by praise or favour. She is anxious that people should set great store by all her deeds and donations. But Grace seeks no reward in time; all the recompense she asks for is God alone, and she wants no more of the things man needs in this life than may serve her to obtain those which are eternal.

14. Nature loves having a crowd of friends and relations, and takes pride in her stately family seat and her distinguished pedigree; she puts on her best smile for those who have influence, says nice things to those with money, and approves of those who share her attitude to life. Grace is different; she loves even her enemies, and does not boast of having a large number of friends. Stately homes and noble birth mean nothing to her, unless she finds greater holiness there. It is the poor she favours rather than the rich; simple, good people she has more in common with than with the influential; she likes those who say what they mean, not liars. She is always encouraging good people to aim at higher prizes, and by their virtues to grow more and more like the Son of God.

15. It is not long before Nature starts grumbling when things are scarce or when trouble comes; Grace endures poverty as long as it lasts.

16. Nature sees everything from her own selfish point of view; all her struggling and striving are for herself alone.

Grace, on the other hand, refers everything to God, from whom it came in the beginning; she never attributes any good to herself or has the arrogance to presume it to be hers; she does not argue or put her own views before other people's, but in all that touches her senses and her understanding submits to the eternal wisdom and the judgement of God. Nature wants to know secrets and hear news; she loves appearing in public and trying out any number of new sensations; she wants people to know her, wants to do something to win their approval and admiration. Grace, though, cares nothing for news and unusual things; she knows that all that kind of thing comes from man's corruption of old, for there is nothing new upon earth, nothing that may last. So this is the lesson she teaches you: to control your senses, and shun foolish self-conceit and boastfulness; to be humble enough to hide anything which might justly earn men's praise and admiration and to seek in all you do, all you enrich your knowledge with, not only your own betterment, but also the honour and glory of God. She has no wish to advertise herself and her deeds, but her desire is that God may be blessed in his gifts, all of which he showers on men simply for love.

17. This Grace is a supernatural light, a kind of special gift of God. It is the peculiar seal of those whom God has chosen, and a pledge of eternal salvation, lifting a man up from the things of earth to love the things of heaven, making a spiritual man of a worldling. You see, then, that the more Nature is kept down and overcome, the greater is the grace that floods a man's soul; and every day, as fresh streams of grace come to him, his inner self is being remoulded, until he takes on the likeness of God.

Chapter 55

ON THE CORRUPTION OF NATURE,
AND THE POWER OF GOD'S GRACE

The Learner: O Lord my God, you have made me in your own image and likeness; grant me this grace, which, as you have shewn, is so great a one, so necessary if I am to be saved: the grace of overcoming my own evil propensities, which drag me into sin and the loss of my soul. I am aware in my body of the authority of sin, opposing the authority of my mind, leading me away in bondage to give in to my sensual inclinations in many a way. I cannot resist its fierce promptings unless your holy grace comes to my rescue, filling my heart with its fiery glow.

2. Yes, I need your grace, and a lot of it at that, if I am to overcome nature, always bent on evil from youth upwards. It was through Adam, the first man, that it fell and was spoiled by sin; and the penalty for that blemish upon humanity has come down upon all men. That very nature which, as made by you, was good and upright, now stands for something vicious, for the weakness of a nature given over to corruption; that is because its instincts, left to themselves, drag the man in whom it has found towards evil and base desires. What little strength has remained is like a little spark hidden among ashes. This is natural reason itself, which, though shut in by intense darkness, can still tell good from evil, still separate truth from falsehood. Yet it is powerless to carry out all it approves of, and now no longer possesses the full light of truth nor the wholesome affections it once had.

3. Thus it comes about, my God, that I take pleasure in your law as far as my inner self is concerned: I know that what you command will be good, just and holy, bidding me shun any kind of evil and sin. Yet with my body I serve the powers of evildoing, by listening to my sensual feelings rather than to reason. Hence, though the will to do good is within me, I cannot find the strength to obey it.

169

Another result is that, although I am always making good resolutions, yet through lack of grace to help my weakness, I recoil in failure at the least sign of opposition. Again, I know the way of perfection and can see perfectly clearly how I ought to behave; but the weight of my own corruption lies heavy on me, and I cannot rise to heights of greater perfection.

4. Lord, your grace is absolutely necessary for me for starting off some good act, for improving it, for making it perfect. Without it I can do nothing; in you, and with the support of your grace, I can do anything. Ah yes, grace is something from heaven; without it, our own merits are nothing, our natural gifts of no account whatever. Skill, wealth, beauty, courage, ability, eloquence—all these have no value in your eyes, Lord, unless grace goes with them. The gifts of nature are shared by good and bad alike, whereas grace, or love, is given especially to God's chosen; those who bear its mark are thought worthy of eternal life. This grace holds so high a position that not even the gift of prophecy, nor the working of miracles, nor the highest reaches of mystical vision are worth anything apart from it. Why, not even faith, hope and the other virtues are acceptable to you without love and grace.

5. It is indeed a blessed thing, grace; it makes the poor in spirit rich in virtues, the man of many riches humble of heart. Ah, come, come down to me and fill me with your comfort, like dew at morning, if you would not have my soul faint with weariness and spiritual drought! Lord, I beg that I may find favour in your sight; your favour, your grace, is enough for me, even if I fail to obtain those other things that nature thirsts for. No matter how many trials and troubles afflict me, I will fear no evil, so long as your grace is with me; it is my strength, bringing me counsel and help, mightier than all my enemies, wiser than all who are wise.

6. It is your grace that teaches us the truth, tells us what rule of life to follow, brings light to our hearts and comfort in our troubles; it drives away sadness, washes away fear,

feeds our devotion and moves us to tears of repentance. Without it, what am I but a tree without rain, a useless bit of timber fit only to be thrown out? So let your grace, Lord, always go in front of me and behind me, to keep me constantly in mind of good deeds to be done; through Jesus Christ, your Son. Amen.

Chapter 56

WE MUST DENY OURSELVES AND
FOLLOW CHRIST ALONG THE WAY OF THE CROSS

The Beloved: The more you can leave yourself behind, my son, the more you will be able to enter into me. Just as desiring no outward pleasure gives you inward peace, so does the surrender of your inmost self unite you with God. I want you to learn perfect self-denial, to obey my will without argument or complaint. Follow me: *I am the Way, the Truth and the Life.*[1] Without a way, a road, there can be no going along it; without truth, no object of knowledge; without life, no living. I am the way you must take, the truth you must believe, the life you must hope for. I am the way that cannot become uncertain, the truth that cannot fail, the life that will never end. I am of all ways the straightest, I am the supreme truth, I am the true life, the blessed life, the life that never was made. If you keep to my way, you will know the truth, and the truth will bring you deliverance; and so you will have eternal life within your grasp.

2. *If you have a mind to enter into life, keep the commandments*[2]; if you want to know the truth, believe me. *If you have a mind to be perfect, go and sell all that belongs to you;*[3] if you want to be my disciple, deny yourself. If you want to possess the life of bliss, despise this present life. If you would be high in heaven, be lowly in this world. If you want to rule beside me, carry the cross at my side; it is only

[1] John 14. 6. [2] Matt. 19. 17. [3] Matt. 19. 21.

171

those who are servants of the cross who find the road to happiness and unfeigning light.

3. *The Learner:* Lord Jesus, your life upon earth was known to but few, and the world sneered at it; grant that I may be like you in bearing the world's scorn; *a disciple is no better than his master, a servant than his lord.*[1] Let this servant of yours make your life his constant study; it is there that I find my salvation, and real holiness. Anything else that I read or hear of can neither feed my soul nor delight me so fully.

4. *The Beloved:* My son, you know about these things, you have read about them; if you put them into practice, you will be blessed. *The man who loves me is the man who keeps the commandments he has from me . . . and I too will love him, and will reveal myself to him;*[2] and I will make him sit down beside me in the kingdom of my Father.

5. *The Learner:* Lord Jesus, let what you have said and promised come true for me; let me earn what you have promised. I have taken the cross, look, taken it from your hands; I will carry it as you have laid it upon me, carry it until death. The life of a good monk is indeed a cross, but it leads him to heaven. We have made a start; we may not go back now, must not desert.

6. So come on, brothers, let us advance together; Jesus will be with us. It is for the sake of Jesus that we have taken up this cross; for his sake let us keep on with it to the end. He will help us, for he has gone before us to be our guide. See where that King of ours goes forth in front of us; he will be fighting at our side. Let us be men, and follow him, and none of us skulk in terror; let us be ready to die bravely in battle, and not sully our glory by abandoning the standard of the cross.

[1] Matt. 10. 24.   [2] John 14. 21.

172

Chapter 57

A MAN SHOULD NOT BE TOO DEPRESSED WHEN HE SLIPS INTO SOME FAULT OR OTHER

The Beloved: I am better pleased, my son, when you are patient and humble in time of trouble than when you feel much comfort and devotion because things are going well. Why do you get so upset when something not altogether kind is said about you? It might well have been worse, but even so you shouldn't let it make you miserable. However, what has upset you now is nothing much; just let it go by. It isn't the first time it's happened, something new to you; and if you live to any age at all, it won't be the last. You can play the man well enough, so long as no opposition crosses your path. You can give good advice, too, and are expert in supporting other people with words of encouragement; but when trouble suddenly turns up on your own doorstep, your good advice and moral support fail you. You ought to remember how little it takes to crush you; you will often have found the truth of that, whenever you have been in the least put out by something. Yet it is to further the cause of your salvation that you have things like that happening to you.

2. As best you can, make sure it does not prey on your mind. It may have hit you, but don't let it send you sprawling in despair, don't let it keep you in its toils for months on end. At least bear it with patience, if you can't manage to do so cheerfully. The offensive remark may not make very pleasant hearing for you, and you may feel furious at it; all the same, you must keep control of yourself. Otherwise, you might let slip some expressions ill-befitting the mouth that spoke them, and Christ's little ones find your words an obstacle in their path to heaven. Those billows of rage will soon calm down, and grace will return to soothe your smarting feelings. I live in readiness to help you—it is your Lord telling you this—in readiness to comfort you more than I have before; all you have to do is to trust and call on me with devotion.

173

3. Be readier to endure; steel yourself to undergo greater affliction. Don't imagine everything is lost, just because you often find yourself in trouble or the prey of grave temptations. You are a man, not God, after all; no angel, but flesh and blood. How do you think you could always stay in the same state of virtue, when Lucifer in heaven couldn't do that, or the first man in Eden? I am he who raises up and supports those who are in distress, lifting up to my Godhead those who are aware of their own weakness.

4. *The Learner:* Bless you, Lord, for those words of yours! They taste sweeter in my mouth than honey and the honeycomb. Whatever should I do in trials and troubles as great as mine are, if I hadn't the support of your holy words? If only I get to the safety of heaven's harbour at last, what do I care what I go through, or how much? Let my ending be a good one, Lord, my passing from this world a happy one. Keep me in mind, O my God, and guide me straight to your kingdom. Amen.

Chapter 58

ABOUT GOD'S SECRETS; WE OUGHT NOT TO SEARCH INTO HIS UNFATHOMABLE JUDGEMENTS

The Beloved: You must beware, my son, of arguing about matters above your understanding, about the unfathomable judgements of God, wondering why one man is so forsaken, while another enjoys such an abundance of God's favour; or why A is so greatly afflicted, and B raised to such extraordinary heights. All these things are quite above anything the human mind can grasp; no amount of reasoning or argument can explain why God does this or that. So when the Enemy puts such questions in your mind, or when you get inquisitive people asking them, answer them in the words of the Prophet: *So just, Lord, you are, your awards so truly given!*[1] You can say this, too: *How unerring are the*

[1] Ps. 118. 137.

awards which the Lord makes, one and all giving proof of their justice![1] My judgements are to be held in awe, not made a subject for discussion; they are beyond the reach of man's understanding.

2. Another thing you must not do is to enquire into the merits of the Saints and argue about them, wondering if one of them was holier than another, or which of them is greater in the kingdom of heaven. Such discussions are often the cause of quarrels and futile arguments, and add fuel to pride and pointless boasting. From these in turn spring envy and ill-feeling, with one man proudly trying to give the prize to one Saint, and the next man doing the same for a different one. Wanting to know such things, to probe into them, is a completely barren occupation, and certainly won't find favour with the Saints themselves; remember, *God is the author of peace, not of disorder,*[2] and that peace is to be found in genuine humility, not in putting oneself on a pedestal.

3. There are some people who are drawn by an emotional kind of piety to have a greater devotion to this Saint or that, but such devotion is human rather than divine. It was I who made all the Saints; I gave them grace and bestowed glory upon them. I know the merits of each one of them; I went before them with the blessings of my loving kindness. Before time was I already knew those beloved of mine; it was I who chose them out of the world, not they who first chose me. I called them by means of my grace, and through my mercy I drew them to me; and in all kinds of temptations I led them as their guide. I poured consolation upon them with unstinting hand, gave them the grace to keep on to the end, and awarded them a crown for their patient endurance.

4. I know them all, the greatest and the least, and in love beyond all reckoning I clasp them to my heart. In all my Saints I am to be praised, and above all things blessed and honoured in each of those whom, without any previous merit of their own, I predestined to have the glory and greatness I have now given them. If anyone, therefore,

[1] Ps. 18. 10. [2] 1 Cor. 14. 33.

speaks slightingly of one of the least of my Saints, he is not
thereby honouring one of my great ones, because I have
made both little and great; and anyone who is lacking in
respect for any of my Saints, is lacking in respect for me too,
and for all others who are in the kingdom of heaven. They
are a single entity, each being bound to the rest by the
bonds of love; all share the same thoughts, the same desires,
all love one another.

5. Not only this, but something higher still; they love
me more than themselves and their own merits. Carried
beyond themselves, drawn forth from their love of self,
they devote themselves entirely to loving me, in whom they
find their rest and their fulfilment. There is nothing that
can turn them away from me or make them grieve, for they
are full of the eternal truth and burn with the unquenchable
fire of love. So let worldly and sensual men stop discussing
the relative positions of the Saints; people like that have no
idea of love beyond what gives them personal pleasure.
They give one Saint a lower place, another a higher one,
just as suits their own preference, and not as the eternal
truth has decided that things really are.

6. In a lot of people, of course, this is just a question of
ignorance, especially in those who have little spiritual
insight and are seldom able to love anyone with a perfect
spiritual love. Such people are still greatly attracted towards one person or another by natural affection and the
liking one man has for another; that is the way they behave in the case of people on earth, and they imagine they
can do the same kind of thing with those who are in heaven.
However, there is an immense gulf between the fancies of
such imperfect men and the view of reality granted to men of
spiritual perception through that lifting of the veil they
have from God.

7. Beware, then, my son, of spending your time delving
into matters like that, matters which outstrip your understanding; if you want an occupation and something to aim
at, let it be an endeavour to be reckoned among the least in
the kingdom of God. Even if anyone *did* know which

Saints were holier than the others, or who was accounted greatest in the kingdom of heaven, what good would that knowledge do him, unless it made him humbler in my sight and caused him to rise from his knees to give greater glory to my name? The man who considers how great his sins are, and how small his virtues, the man who realizes how far he lags behind the perfection of the Saints, is acting in a way far more pleasing to God than the man who has arguments about which of the Saints are greater or lesser in God's sight. It is better to beg help of the Saints with devout prayers and tears, and humbly to call upon them for their glorious intercession, than to indulge a foolish curiosity by trying to learn their secrets.

8. The Saints are completely and utterly contented; if only men knew the way to contentment, and could restrain their empty chatter! The Saints take no pride in their own merits, attribute no goodness to themselves, but all to me; it was I who gave them everything out of my boundless love. They are brimming with so great a love of God, so overflowing a joy, that nothing is wanting to their glory, and nothing can be lacking to complete their happiness. The higher they are in glory, the humbler are all my Saints in themselves, the closer and dearer to me. That is what is meant by that passage in Holy Scripture: *they threw down their crowns before God, falling prostrate before the Lamb, and worshipped him who lives for ever and ever.*[1]

9. A lot of people want to know who is greatest in the kingdom of God, even though they don't know whether they themselves will ever be worthy to be counted among the least there. It is a great thing even to be among the least in heaven, where all are great; because all there shall be called, and shall really be, the children of God. The least there shall be equal to a thousand ordinary men, and the sinner, for all his hundred years, shall die. When the disciples asked who was greatest in the kingdom of heaven, this was the reply they heard: *Unless you become like little children again, you shall not enter the kingdom of heaven. He is greatest in*

[1] *Cf.* Apoc. 4. 10.

the kingdom of heaven who will abase himself like this little child.[1]

10. It will go ill with those who disdain to abase themselves willingly to the level of little children; the door of the heavenly kingdom is low and will not let them in. Those with money, too, will be sorry, the men who have their own kind of comfort in this world; the poor will enter the kingdom of God, while they themselves stand whimpering outside. So be glad, you humble folk, dance for joy, you who are poor; it is to you the kingdom of God belongs, if only you will walk by the paths of truth.

Chapter 59

ALL OUR HOPE AND TRUST
MUST BE PLACED IN GOD ALONE

The Learner: Lord, what can I rely on in this life? What is my greatest comfort of all that can be seen under heaven? Is it not you, my Lord and my God, you whose mercy is beyond reckoning? Where have things gone well with me, with you not there? And when could things have gone badly for me, with you at my side? I had rather be poor for your sake than rich without you. I would choose to roam the world with you beside me than possess heaven and not you; but heaven is where you are, and where you are not—that is what death is, and hell. It is for you that I long; it is this longing that constrains me to sigh for you, to call out to you, to beg you for help. Finally, there is no one I can trust unreservedly, no one who in my need will help me at just the right moment, but you alone, my God. You are my hope, my trust, my comfort, always standing by me whatever happens.

2. All men seek their own advantage; all *your* scheming, Lord, is for my salvation, my betterment. Under your

[1] Matt. 18. 3, 4.

178

hands, everything turns out to be for my good. You may let me in for all sorts of trials and troubles, but you arrange for things to happen in that way only for my own good. Testing them in all sorts of fashions is a way you have of dealing with those whom you love; so when you test me like that I ought to love you and praise you just as much as if you were filling me with your heavenly consolation.

3. It is in you, then, Lord God, that I put all my hope, to you that I run for protection; in your hands I put all my troubles and misery. If I look at anything apart from you for help, I find nothing but uncertainty and doubtful stability. Having a lot of friends won't help me, having influential people to back me won't further my cause. If I ask the wise for advice, they can give me no answer I can act on; there can be no comfort for me in the books of the learned. No precious substance can buy my freedom, no private paradise afford me shelter. No, Lord, none of these can help me unless you yourself stand by me, helping me, strengthening and comforting me, instructing and keeping watch over me.

4. When you are not with me, everything that seems likely to bring me peace and happiness means nothing to me; things like that don't really make me happy. You are the goal for which all good men are striving; you are the highest peak of all that has life, the lowest deep that underlies all speech. Nothing is so great a comfort to your servants as to trust in you above all else. It is to you, my God, I raise my eyes, in you, O Father of mercies, that I place my trust. Bless and make holy this soul of mine with your heavenly blessing; so let it become a place sacred enough for you to dwell in it, a place where your eternal glory may stay for ever. Let nothing be found in this temple of your greatness on which your royal glance might light with disfavour. In the immensity of your goodness, the unmeasured stores of your mercy, look upon me and listen to the prayer of this poor servant of yours, so far from home here in the land of the shadow of death. Guard and keep the soul of this least of your servants amid the many

dangers of this uncertain life. Give me your grace for my companion, and guide me along the path of peace, until I reach my true country, the land of unending light. Amen.

BOOK IV

ABOUT THE BLESSED SACRAMENT

A DEVOUT ENCOURAGEMENT
TO RECEIVE HOLY COMMUNION

THE VOICE OF CHRIST

Come to me, all you that labour and are burdened; I will give you rest.[1] *What is this bread which I am to give? It is my flesh, given for the life of the world.*[2] *Take, eat; this is my body, given up for you. Do this for a commemoration of me.*[3] *He who eats my flesh, and drinks my blood, lives continually in me, and I in him. The words I have been speaking to you are spirit, and life.*[4]

Chapter 1

ON THE DEEP REVERENCE
WITH WHICH CHRIST IS TO BE RECEIVED

The Learner: O Christ, the everlasting Truth, all these are sayings of yours, although they were not all spoken on one occasion or written down in a single passage. Since, then, they are yours, and since they are true, it is for me to welcome them all with faith and gratitude. Your sayings they are; it was you who spoke them; mine, too, because it was for my salvation that you uttered them. Gladly do I take them from your lips, that they may be implanted all the more firmly in my heart. So kindly those words of yours are, so full of sweetness and love, they stir my soul; but my own sins fill me with fear, my troubled conscience flails me when I would receive so great a mystery. The sweetness of your words calls me on, but my clustering sins weigh me down.

[1] Matt. 11. 28. [2] John 6. 52. [3] Matt. 26. 26; 1 Cor. 11. 24. [4] John 6. 57, 64.

2. You bid me approach you in faith, if I would share what is yours; to receive the food of immortality, if I desire to win glory and life everlasting. *Come to me*, you say, *all you that labour and are burdened; I will give you rest.* O Lord, my God, how sweet and friendly do those words sound in the ear of a sinner! those words in which you invite the poor and the needy to the Communion of your most holy body! But, Lord, who am I to dare approach you? Why, the heaven of heavens cannot contain you; and yet you say, "Come to me, all of you".

3. What is the meaning of so loving a disregard of your dignity, so friendly an invitation? How shall I dare come? I know of no good in me that might give me grounds so to presume. How shall I bring you into my home, I who so many a time have wronged your immense kindness to me? Angels and Archangels bow down before you, Saints and holy people stand in dread of you; and yet you say, "Come to me, all of you".

If it were not you, Lord, saying these words, who would believe them? If it were not your own command, who would dare draw near?

4. That good man Noe toiled for a hundred years, building the ark, that he and a few besides might be saved; then how shall I, in a single hour, fit myself to receive with proper respect the creator of the world? Your great servant Moses, that special friend of yours, made an ark of imperishable wood, decking it with the finest gold, in order to place the Tablets of the Law inside; and shall I, perishable creature that I am, dare so easily to receive you, the framer of the law, the giver of life? Solomon, wisest of the kings of Israel, gave seven years to building a magnificent temple in praise of your name; for eight days he kept the feast of its dedication; a thousand victims he sacrificed as peace-offerings, and amid joyous applause and the braying of trumpets he solemnly took the ark of the covenant to the place made ready for it: and shall I, poorest and most wretched of men, bring you into my home, I who know how to spend scarce half an hour devoutly? I wish I

could spend even half an hour as it ought to be spent!

5. Ah, my God, how much did those men strive to do to win your regard! And how little it is that I do; how short a time I take in preparing to make my Communion! Rarely am I completely recollected; rarely indeed am I entirely free from distraction. In the saving presence of your Godhead, no unseemly thought should arise, nothing created should take hold of my mind; for he who is to enter the guest-room of my heart is not an angel, but the angels' very Lord.

6. And yet how great a difference there is between the ark of the covenant and its relics, and your spotless body and its mighty powers, powers that beggar speech; between those sacrifices of the Old Law, the pattern of that which was to come, and the true victim of your body, the fulfilment of those sacrifices of old.

7. Then why is my heart not more aflame at your wondrous presence? Why don't I take greater care in preparing to receive your holy gift, seeing that those holy patriarchs and prophets of old, those kings and princes, together with all their people, shewed such great devotion for divine worship?

8. David, that most devout of kings, danced with all his might before the ark of God, when he recalled the kindnesses bestowed of old upon his forefathers; he devised all sorts of musical instruments and wrote psalms, which he taught his people to sing with gladness; he himself, too, often sang to the harp, when moved by the grace of the Holy Spirit. He taught the people of Israel to praise God with all their heart, to join each day in blessing him and telling of his goodness. If people in those days performed such acts of devotion, recalling the praise of God before the ark of the covenant, how great today should be the homage and devotion paid by me and by all Christian people in the presence of the Blessed Sacrament, and in receiving the most worshipful body of Christ?

9. There are many people who run off to various places to see relics of Saints; filled with wonder on hearing of their

deeds, they look over the vast churches enshrining them and kiss the holy bones in their setting of silk and gold; and here you are before me on the altar, you, my God, the Saint of Saints, the maker of men, the Lord of the Angels. When men go to see such things it is often out of curiosity and a wish for change of scenery; they come back little inclined to amend their lives, especially when their pilgrimage has been a mere light-hearted dashing hither and thither, without any real touching of the heart. But here in the Sacrament of the altar you, my God, are wholly present, you, the man Christ Jesus. There we are dowered in abundance with the fruit of eternal salvation, every time that we receive you worthily and devoutly. It is not frivolity that draws us there, not curiosity, not a desire for sensual pleasure, but firm faith, devout hope and love unfeigned.

10. How wonderful are your ways with us, O God, unseen maker of the world! How sweet and gracious your dealings with your chosen, when you offer yourself to them to be received in this Sacrament! It goes beyond all that the understanding can grasp; for devout souls it has a unique attraction, kindling in them the flames of love. Those who are truly faithful to you, who spend the whole of their lives trying to mend their faults, receive from this most adorable Sacrament the grace of devotion and the love of virtue.

11. Wonderful indeed is the grace that comes from this Sacrament, wonderful and hidden. It is only the faithful followers of Christ that know it; those who have no faith, those who are the slaves of sin, can have no conception of it. In this Sacrament we receive the gift of spiritual grace; the soul's lost strength is renewed, and the beauty that sin had marred returns to it once more. Indeed, so powerful is the grace of this Sacrament, so full the outpouring of devotion, that sometimes not only the mind but even the feeble body is aware that greater strength has been given it.

12. How great a pity it is, how much a matter for regret, that we are so lukewarm, so careless; that we are not drawn to receive Christ with greater love. For in him lies all the hope, all the merit, of those who are to be saved. It is he

who makes us holy, he who redeems us; he who comforts us on our earthly journey, he who is the everlasting bliss of the Saints. Yes, a great pity it is that many have such scant regard for this saving mystery, which fills heaven with joy and keeps the whole creation in being. How blind men are, how hard their hearts, not to pay greater attention to so wondrous a gift as this! It even happens that their daily Communions become a mere formal routine.

13. Suppose that this most holy Sacrament were celebrated in one place only; suppose there were only one priest in the whole world to say the words of consecration. How men would long to go to that place, to visit that one priest of God and see the divine mysteries celebrated! But now there are many priests, and in many places Christ is offered, so that the further afield Holy Communion is spread throughout the world, the greater proof it may yield of God's grace and love for men. Thank you, O good Jesus, eternal shepherd, for deigning to refresh us poor outcasts with your precious body and blood; for inviting us with your own lips to partake of this mystery, when you say: *Come to me, all you that labour and are burdened; I will give you rest.*

Chapter 2

ON THE GREAT GOODNESS AND LOVE SHEWN BY GOD TO MAN IN THIS SACRAMENT

The Learner: Trusting in your goodness, Lord, in your great mercy, I come in my sickness to him who can make me well; hungered and athirst, I come to the fountain of life, a beggar to the King of Heaven, a servant to his Lord, a creature to his Creator, one lonely and sad to him who loves and consoles me. But what have I done to deserve that you should come to me? Who am I, that you should make me a gift of yourself? Dare I, a sinner, appear before you? And do you forget your greatness and come to a sinner? You know this servant of yours; you know nothing good of him, to make him deserve this gift at your hands. I do not hide my wretchedness; I acknowledge your goodness, I praise your kindness, I thank you for your overwhelming love. It is for your own sake that you do this, not for any merit of mine. It is to make your goodness better known to me, to bestow your love more fully upon me, to give me a more wondrous example of humility. Since, then, it pleases you so to deal with me, since you have commanded that things should be so, it pleases me in my turn that you should so stoop to my lowliness; and I hope that my sinfulness may not stand as a barrier between us.

2. O Jesus, sweetest, kindest, what great worship and thanksgiving we ought to shew you, what never-ending praise, in return for the gift of your holy body! There is not a man to be found able to unfold in words its wonderful power. But what shall my thoughts be of as I make this Communion of mine, as I draw near to my Lord? To worship him as I ought is beyond my power, and yet I long to receive him devoutly. What better thought can I have, what thought more profitable for my soul's health, than this: to abase myself entirely before you and to praise your boundless goodness towards me? I praise you, O my God, I give you glory for ever. Myself I look on with scorn and place at your feet, in the depths of my nothingness.

3. Look, Lord, you are the Saint of all Saints, and I but a filthy sinner; you bend down to me, because I am not worthy to lift my gaze towards you. Yes, you come to me; you want to be with me; you invite me to your feast. You wish to give me heavenly food to eat, the *Bread of Angels*[1]: your own self, no less, that living bread which came down from heaven and gives life to the world.

4. See where love has its source, see how brightly shines this divine abasement! How deep should our thanks be, how sincere our praise, for this your gift. It was indeed a device to heal and profit our souls, when you brought this

[1] Ps. 77. 2.

Sacrament into being; a sweet and joyous banquet indeed, in which you gave yourself to be our food. What wonderful things you do, Lord! How mighty your power is, how unfailing your truth! You gave the word, and everything came into being; so was it with this Sacrament, because it was you who so gave command.

5. How wonderful a thing it is, worthy of man's belief, yet exceeding the grasp of his mind, that you, my Lord and my God, truly God and truly man, are wholly contained beneath the lowly shape of bread and wine; that you are eaten by him who receives you, and yet not consumed. You, the Lord of all things, who stand in need of nothing, have wished to live in our midst by means of this Sacrament. Keep my heart and my body free from stain, so that with a glad and untroubled conscience I may take part more frequently in this mystery of yours; and may I receive to my eternal salvation this Sacrament that you have blessed and devised to be for your own particular honour, your everlasting keepsake.

6. Be glad, my soul; thank God for leaving behind for you in this vale of tears so precious a gift as this is, so matchless a comfort. For every time you consider this mystery and receive the body of Christ you are furthering the work of your redemption and partaking in all the merits of Christ. There is never any lessening of the love Christ has for us, never a running dry of the stream of his pitiful intercession on our behalf. What you ought to do, then, is to prepare yourself each time for this Sacrament by thinking of it afresh, by pondering with careful consideration the great mystery of salvation. Whenever you say Mass or hear it, it ought to seem to you as great, as unexpected and as joyful a thing as if that same day Christ had first come down into the Virgin's womb and become man; as if he were hanging on the cross, suffering and dying for the salvation of men.

Chapter 3

ON THE ADVANTAGE OF FREQUENT COMMUNION

The Learner: Look, Lord, I have come to you here to benefit from your gift, to be gladdened by that holy feast of
yours, that feast which in your kindness you have made
ready for the poor, O my God. In you is everything that I
can or should desire; you are my salvation and my redemption, my hope and my strength, my honour and my glory.
Then comfort today *your servant's heart, this heart that
aspires to you, Lord Jesus.*[1] I long now to receive you with
devotion and reverence; I would fain shew you into my
home. So may I deserve, like Zaccheus of old, to win your
blessing and to be assigned a place among the children of
Abraham. My soul longs for your body; my heart is
athirst to become one with you.

2. Give me yourself—that is all I want; apart from you
there is nothing able to bring me comfort. Without you I
cannot exist; without these visits of yours I cannot live.
That is why I must often approach you and receive you as
medicine that brings health to my soul; if not, I shall faint
by the wayside, deprived of this heavenly food. Yours is a
heart overflowing with pity, my Jesus; when you were
preaching to the people and healing their manifold diseases,
you said once: *I must not send them away fasting, or perhaps they will grow faint on their journey.*[2] So deal with me
as you did with them; it was to comfort those faithful to
you that you left your presence behind in this Sacrament.
You are the soul's sweet refreshment; the man who receives
you worthily will share by inheritance the everlasting glory.
But how often I slip into sin; how quickly I grow dull of
heart and neglectful! That is why it is vital for me to freshen
myself, to clean myself, to stir the fire in my heart by frequent prayer and confession. If I neglect these means too
long, I may fall away from my good resolutions.

3. A man's senses have a twist towards evil from his

[1] Ps. 85. 4. [2] Matt. 15. 32.

youth upward; without the help of this divine medicine, he soon starts slipping into bigger sins. It is Holy Communion that drags him away from evil and gives him strength to remain good. I am often careless and lukewarm now, when I say Mass or go to Communion; what would it be like if I didn't take this remedy, if I neglected to seek the great help it gives me? I may not be fit to say Mass every day, may not be in the right dispositions; but I will make it my business to receive the divine mysteries at suitable times and make ready to share in the great grace they bestow. This is the chief comfort of the faithful soul, all the time it is journeying apart from you in this mortal body: oftentimes to remember its God and with devout heart to welcome her Beloved within her.

4. Lord God, you who give being and life to all souls, how wonderful is the way in which your love stoops to our lowliness! You do not think it below you to come to a poor, unworthy soul and to appease her hunger with the fullness of your Godhead and your manhood alike! Happy the mind, blessed the soul, that deserves reverently to receive you, her Lord and her God, and in receiving you to be filled with spiritual gladness! How great a Lord is he whom she receives, how beloved a guest; how pleasant a companion, how faithful a friend! How beauteous and noble a spouse she embraces, one that surpasses all other loves, one to be loved more than all that tempts our desire. O my beloved, my most sweet Jesus, let heaven and earth fall silent before you, with all their lovely adornment; whatever they have that makes us praise and admire them is but granted to them by your unstinting kindness; they fall far short of the beauty of your name, you whose wisdom is beyond all reckoning.

Chapter 4

ON THE MANY BENEFITS ACCORDED TO THOSE WHO COMMUNICATE DEVOUTLY

The Learner: O Lord my God, so guide this servant of yours with the blessings of your kindness that I may deserve to approach this your Sacrament with due devotion. Stir up my heart to meet you; strip from me the sloth that weighs upon me. Visit me with your healing presence; let me taste in spirit that sweetness of yours which, as in a fountain, gushes unseen in this Sacrament. Give light to my eyes; enable me to gaze on this great mystery. Give me strength to believe it with unwavering faith. What takes place is your doing; it is brought about by no power of man. It is your own holy institution, not something man has invented. Nowhere will you find a man capable by himself of grasping and understanding these things; they elude even the fine intelligence of the angels. Then what about me, who am an unworthy sinner, nothing but dust and ashes? How can I examine, how grasp so deep, so holy a mystery?

2. Lord, with honesty of intent, with firm good faith and at your bidding I come to you full of hope and adoration; I really do believe you are present here in this Sacrament, both God and man. It is your wish that I should receive you, to become one with you in love. It is for this that I beg for your mercy, earnestly asking you to give me a special grace; let me dissolve and be one with you; let me overflow with your love; let me henceforth allow entrance to no comfort but such as comes from you. This most high and adorable Sacrament is the health of body and soul, the remedy for every spiritual disease. By it my vices are cured, my passions bridled, my temptations overcome or diminished; grace is poured out more lavishly in my soul, budding virtue made to bloom, faith made firm, hope strengthened and love set afire and spread abroad.

3. O my God, keeper of my soul, restorer of human frailty and giver of all inward consolation, many are the

blessings you have showered in this Sacrament, many and frequent the blessings you shower still on the souls you love when they make a devout Communion. Great is the comfort you give them against all sorts of trouble; from the depths of their despondency you lift them up and give them hope in your protection; and with fresh grace you cheer and enlighten their hearts. Thus it is that those who before Communion felt distressed and lacking in love find themselves afterwards changed for the better, now that they have been refreshed by that heavenly meat and drink. In so dealing with your chosen you have a purpose. It is to make them conscious of the truth, by their own plain experience, that by themselves they are extremely weak, and that from you they gain an immense store of goodness and grace. They learn that by themselves they are cold, hard-hearted and lacking in devotion, but after receiving you they gain in fervour, eagerness and devout affection. Who that comes humbly to the fountain of sweetness does not take away with him a little of its sweetness? Who can stand by a roaring fire and not feel something of its heat? And you are a fountain ever brimming and overflowing, a fire perpetually burning and never extinguished.

4. So, then, if I may not draw from the fullness of this fountain, may not drink till my thirst is utterly slaked, yet will I put my mouth to a hole in this heavenly pipe; so may I catch from it a tiny drop to allay my thirst and prevent my being parched within.

If I cannot yet become a creature of heaven, aflame with love, like the Cherubim and Seraphim, I will at least try to be earnest at my devotions and make ready my heart, so that by humbly receiving this life-giving Sacrament I may catch a spark, be it never so little, of the divine fire. O good Jesus, O most holy Saviour, do you of your kindness and grace make up for me whatever in me may be wanting; for you did not disdain to call all men to you, when you said: *Come to me, all you that labour and are burdened; I will give you rest.*[1]

[1] Matt. 11. 28.

5. Labour? Yes, I labour in the sweat of my brow; I am tormented by anguish of heart, weighed down by my sins, troubled by temptations, entangled and oppressed by many an evil passion. There is no one to help me, no one to bring me to freedom and safety but you, Lord God, my Saviour. To you I entrust myself and all that is mine, that you may keep me and bring me to life everlasting. Take me, for the praise and glory of your name, you who have given me your body and your blood to be my meat and drink. Grant, O Lord God my Saviour, that through often receiving your mysteries my sense of devotion may grow ever greater.

Chapter 5

ON THE DIGNITY OF THE SACRAMENT AND ON THE PRIESTLY OFFICE

The Beloved: Though you had the purity of the Angels and the holiness of St John the Baptist, you would not be worthy to receive or handle this Sacrament. It is for no merit of man's that it is man who consecrates and handles the Sacrament of Christ and receives the Bread of Angels as his food. The priesthood is a great mystery; how great a dignity is that of a priest! He has been given powers not granted to angels; for no one but a priest duly ordained in church has the power to say Mass, to consecrate the body of Christ. Now the priest is the agent of God, using God's word as God has commanded and arranged; but it is God himself who is the chief actor, working unseen; to him is subject all that he has willed to be, and all that he has commanded obeys his laws.

2. You should therefore place more faith in Almighty God, respecting this most wonderful Sacrament, than in the evidence of your own senses or in any outward sign. You should approach this task of yours with holy dread. Think what you are; recall whose ministry it was that was

handed down to you when the Bishop laid his hands upon you. Yes, you are a priest, ordained to say Mass; you ought, then, to see that you offer this sacrifice to God faithfully and devoutly and at the proper time, and that the life you lead is one with which no one may find fault. The burden you bear has not been lightened; no, you have bound yourself with fetters of stricter self-discipline, engaged to strive for a higher level of holiness. It is a priest's duty to be adorned with every virtue and to make his own good life an example to others. He ought to spend his days not among the common run of men, but in the company of the Angels in heaven or with men of perfect life upon earth.

3. A priest wearing sacred vestments takes the place of Christ, humbly and earnestly to beseech God for himself and for all his people. Both before him and behind he wears the sign of the cross, to make him continually mindful of the sufferings of Christ. He wears the cross before him on the chasuble that he may gaze earnestly on the steps of Christ and ardently strive to follow them. He wears the sign of the cross behind him that he may bear, without retaliation and for God's sake, whatever injuries are done him by others. He wears the cross in front of him that he may grieve for his own sins, and behind him that he may mourn in sympathy over the misdeeds of others, remembering that he has been set as a go-between betwixt God and the sinner. Let him not grow weary of prayer and of offering the holy sacrifice until he deserves to obtain grace and mercy. When a priest says Mass, he gives honour to God, joy to the Angels, strength to the Church, help to the living, rest to the dead; and he makes himself a sharer in all good things.

Chapter 6

THE QUESTION OF PREPARATION FOR COMMUNION

The Learner: Lord, when I compare your greatness and my own wretchedness. it makes me very much afraid and troubled at heart; because if I fail to approach you, it is from life that I am fleeing, yet if I force myself upon you in an unworthy state, I incur your displeasure. What, then, shall I do, my God, you who are my helper, my counsellor in time of need?

2. Shew me the right way; set before me some short exercise suitable for Holy Communion. That is something profitable for me to know: the way, I mean, to make my heart ready, devoutly and reverently, for receiving your Sacrament to the health of my soul, or for offering so great and divine a sacrifice.

Chapter 7

ON EXAMINING OUR CONSCIENCE AND MAKING A PURPOSE OF AMENDMENT

The Beloved: When a priest of God comes to offer this Sacrament, to handle it or receive it, he should do so above all else with deep abasement of heart and lowly reverence, with unshaken faith and with the loving intention of giving honour to God. Carefully examine your conscience and do your best to cleanse and enlighten it by being truly sorry for your sins and humbly confessing them. Thus you will have no serious sin on your conscience that you know of, nothing to prevent your freely approaching the Sacrament. Be sorry for all yours sins in general, and be particularly remorseful about the faults you commit every day. If there is time, confess to God in your inmost heart how ill-regulated your passions are.

2. You must be full of grief and regret that you are still so attached to the flesh and the world, your passions so unsubdued, your heart so full of the stirrings of evil desire; so unguarded in your outward senses, so often immersed in foolish fancies; so keen on what happens outside you, so careless of your inner life; so lightly given to laughter and levity, so hard when it comes to bewailing your sins; so eager for relaxation and bodily ease, so slothful to do penance and to arouse your zeal for good; so avid for the latest news, for lovely things to look at, so backward in welcoming humiliation and contempt; so anxious to have a lot of possessions, so mean in giving and so stubborn in holding on to things; in speech so heedless, in silence so unrestrained; in manner so disorderly, in action so inconsiderate; so lavish with food, so deaf to the word of God; so swift to take a rest, so slow to be up and doing; so wide-awake for gossip, so drowsy for holy vigils; so much in a hurry to be finished, so wandering in attention; so careless in saying your office, so lukewarm in saying Mass, so wanting in fervour at Communion; so easily distracted, so seldom completely recollected; so easily put out of temper, so ready to take umbrage; so ready to pass judgement, so harsh in rebuke; so cheerful when things go well with you, so despondent when they don't; so often making lots of good resolutions and doing so little to keep them.

3. When you have confessed and grieved for these and all your other failings, sorrowing at heart and deeply deploring your own weakness, firmly resolve that you will ever amend your life and advance to a better state of soul. Then commit yourself entirely to me and with the whole of your will offer yourself on the altar of your heart as an unceasing sacrifice to honour my name. This you can do by faithfully entrusting yourself to me, both body and soul. Thus you will be worthy to approach and offer sacrifice to God and to receive the Sacrament of my body to the health of your soul.

4. There is no worthier offering, no greater means of making amends in order to wash away your sins than to

offer one's self wholly and purely to God, together with the offering of the body of Christ in the Mass and in Communion. If a man does his best and is really sorry for his sins, every time he comes to me for pardon and grace, *all his transgressions shall be forgotten*; they will all receive pardon. *What pleasure should I find in the death of a sinner, the Lord God says, when he might have turned back from his evil ways, and found life instead?*[1]

Chapter 8

ON THE OFFERING OF CHRIST ON THE CROSS, AND OUR OWN SURRENDER

The Beloved: Willingly, with arms outstretched upon the cross where I hung naked, I offered myself to God the Father for your sins, in total surrender, my whole being turned to a sacrifice pleasing to God. So you in your turn should offer yourself to me daily at Mass, with all your powers and affections. A willing offering it ought to be, an offering pure and holy, made with all the power of your inmost heart. There is nothing I ask of you more than this, to strive to surrender yourself entirely to me. I care for nothing that you offer me besides yourself; it is not your gift that I want, it is you. If you had everything else, and had not me, you would be unsatisfied; so it is with me; nothing you give can please me, if you fail to offer yourself. Offer yourself to me and give yourself wholly to God; what you offer will be accepted. You know that I offered myself entirely to the Father for your sake; I gave the whole of my body and my blood to be your food, so that I might be wholly yours and you mine for ever. But if you cling to your own selfhood and do not freely offer yourself to my will, your offering will not be perfect and we shall not be wholly one. So then, before everything you do, you ought willingly to place yourself in God's hands as an offering,

[1] Ezech. 18. 22, 23.

if you desire to win freedom and grace. That is the reason why so few are given inward freedom and enlightenment; they cannot altogether renounce self. What I said once still holds good today: *None of you can be my disciple if he does not take leave of all that he possesses.*[1] Do you, then, if you would be my disciple, offer yourself to me, together with all the powers of your heart.

Chapter 9

WE SHOULD OFFER OURSELVES AND ALL THAT IS OURS TO GOD AND PRAY FOR ALL MEN

The Learner: Lord, everything in heaven is yours, everything on earth. I desire to offer myself to you in willing surrender and to remain yours for ever. Lord, in singleness of heart I offer myself to you today, to be your servant for ever; this I do to shew my allegiance to you, as a sacrifice of everlasting praise. Take me, together with this holy sacrifice of your precious body, this offering that I make you today in the presence of the Angels who stand by unseen; may it further my salvation and that of all your people.

2. Lord, I offer you upon this altar of reconciliation all the sins and wrongdoing I have committed before you and your holy Angels, from the first day I had the power to sin up to this present time; burn and consume them all in the fire of your love; wipe out the stains of my sins; clean my conscience from every misdeed; give me back your grace, which through sin I have lost; grant me full pardon for all my offences, and mercifully receive me with the kiss of peace.

3. There is nothing I can do about my sins but humbly confess and bewail them, and cry without ceasing for your mercy. I beseech you, my God, mercifully hear me, as I stand here before you. All my sins are utterly abhorrent to me; I never want to commit them again. I grieve over them

[1] Luke 14. 33.

and shall grieve as long as I live; and I am ready to do penance for them and to atone for them as best I can. Do away with my sins, O my God, for thy holy name's sake do away with them; save my soul, which you have bought at the price of your precious blood. See, I entrust myself to your mercy, surrender myself into your hands. Deal with me according to your goodness, not according to my malice and sinfulness.

4. I offer you also all my good deeds, pitifully few and unfinished though they be. Do you amend and hallow them; make them pleasing and welcome to you, and ever raise them to greater heights; and bring me, slothful and useless specimen of humanity though I be, to a blessed and worthy end.

5. I offer you also all the devout yearnings of the faithful; the needs of my parents, my friends, my brothers and sisters and all who are dear to me; for those, too, who for love of you have shewn kindness to me or to others; for those who have desired or asked me to pray and say Mass for them and theirs, whether still living in the flesh or gone from this world. May they all be conscious of the approach of your helping grace, the support of your comfort, the withdrawal of pain; freed from all evils, may they duly give you thanks with solemn and joyful praise.

6. I offer you also my prayers and this appeasing sacrifice for those especially who have in any way hurt me, distressed me or spoken against me, or involved me in loss, or given me cause for grievance; for those, too, whom I have at any time distressed or troubled, pained or hindered from good, whether by word or deed, consciously or unawares. Do you forgive us all alike our sins and the hurt we do one another. Lord, take from our hearts all suspicion, ill-temper, anger and dissension and everything else that may be hurtful to charity and lessen brotherly love. Have mercy, Lord, have mercy on those who beg for your mercy; give your grace to those who stand in need of it; make us so to live that we may be worthy to enjoy your grace and make our way to life everlasting. Amen.

Chapter 10

WE SHOULD NOT LIGHTLY
KEEP AWAY FROM HOLY COMMUNION

The Beloved: You must often return to the source of grace and divine mercy, the source of goodness and all purity, to enable you to be cured of your passions and vices; so may you deserve to become stronger and more watchful in repelling all the temptations and deceits of the devil. That enemy of yours is aware of the great profit and remedy for sin contained in Holy Communion; and so in every way and on every occasion he does his utmost to drag faithful and devout souls, as far as he is able, away from the holy table and set up barriers between them and it.

2. There are some people who suffer more grievous assaults from Satan whenever they are making their preparation for Holy Communion. As it is written in the Book of Job, the evil spirit comes among the children of God to trouble them with his usual wicked devices, or make them over-fearful and confused. His aim is to lessen their love or to attack and destroy their faith, so that they will give up Communion altogether or come to it with little fervour. But you must not mind his wiles and his imaginations of evil, however filthy and horrible; fling all those foul pictures of his back at his own head. Treat the wretch with scorn and derision; do not let his assaults or the disturbances he arouses in you make you refrain from going to Communion.

3. What often sets up a barrier is an unreasonable worrying about your feelings of devotion and tormenting thoughts about going to confession. Act on the advice of those who are versed in such things and lay aside your troubling thoughts and scruples; they are a bar to the grace of God and ruin your devotion. Do not refrain from going to Communion because of some little matter that weighs on your mind and perplexes it; go straight off to confession, and freely forgive all the hurt that others have done you.

199

Should you happen to have done a bad turn to someone else, humbly beg pardon, and God will freely grant you forgiveness.

4. What is the point of delaying confession or putting off Holy Communion? Cleanse yourself at once; spit out the poison, make haste to take the antidote, and you will feel better than if you had long delayed to do so. Put off Communion today for some reason or other, and tomorrow something worse may turn up; go on like that, and you may be debarred from Communion for a long while, growing ever less fit to receive it. As soon as you can, shake yourself free of the torpor that weighs on you now; there's not much point in suffering long torments, or going about for ages in a state of distress and keeping away from the sacraments because of difficulties that crop up daily. No, on the contrary, deferring Communion for a long time is extremely harmful; it usually brings about great spiritual stagnation. It is a sad fact that some people, lacking in fervour and self-control, are only too glad to find excuses for putting off their confession. They desire to have their Holy Communion postponed, for fear they should have to keep a stricter watch over their lives.

5. How little love they have, how feeble their devotion, those who so lightly put off going to Holy Communion! Happy the man and well with God who lives such a life, keeps so unspotted a conscience, that he would be ready to communicate every day, and do it gladly, if only he were allowed to do so and could escape remark. If a man sometimes refrains from communicating out of humility or because some lawful cause prevents him, he is to be commended for his reverence; but if it is because sloth has crept over him, he should bestir himself and do his best. God will come to the aid of his desire because of his good intention, on which he looks with special favour.

6. When a man is lawfully prevented from communicating, he still keeps his good will, his devout resolve to receive the Sacrament, and thus he will not be deprived of the benefits it brings. It is within the power of any devout

person, no matter the day or the hour, to approach Christ in spiritual Communion with none to say him nay, and his soul will profit thereby. All the same, you ought on fixed days and definite times to receive the body of the Redeemer sacramentally, with loving reverence, seeking the praise and honour of God rather than your own comfort. Every time you mystically communicate and are given that unseen refreshment, you devoutly recall the mystery of Christ's incarnation and passion; your hearts are kindled with the fire of his love.

7. The man who prepares himself only when a feast is coming or when custom obliges him, will as often as not be quite unprepared.

Happy the man who, every time he says Mass or goes to Communion, offers himself wholly to the Lord. When saying Mass, be neither too long about it nor too hurried; keep to the good balance between the two struck by those with whom you are living. You ought not to induce annoyance and weariness in others, but keep to the ways laid down by your predecessors, better mindful of other people's profit than your own devotion or spiritual taste.

Chapter 11

THE BODY OF CHRIST AND HOLY SCRIPTURE ARE MOST NECESSARY TO THE FAITHFUL SOUL

The Learner: Jesus, my most sweet Lord, how great is the sweetness enjoyed by the faithful soul who feasts in your company and at your banquet; there no other food is set before her than you, her only beloved, one to be desired above all the desires of her heart. How sweet it would be for me, could I but weep before you, from the depth of the love within me, and with the devout Magdalen bathe your feet with my tears! But where is that devotion? Where that unstinted outpouring of holy tears? Surely, here before

201

THE IMITATION OF CHRIST

you and your holy Angels, my heart should be wholly
aflame; I ought to be weeping for very joy, for here in this
Sacrament I have you truly present, though hidden
beneath another form.

2. Were I to gaze upon you in the blinding light of your
Godhead, my eyes could not stand the sight; why, the
whole world itself could not stay unmoved beneath the
splendour, the glory of your majesty. It is out of consideration for my weakness that you veil yourself beneath this
Sacrament. Here I truly hold, here I adore, him whom the
angels adore in heaven; I, as yet, by faith alone, they as he
really is, with no veil between. I must be content with the
light of true faith, walking by its rays until the dawning of
the day of everlasting glory, when the shadows of outward
seeming shall move away. But *when the time of fulfilment
comes,*[1] there will be an end of using Sacraments; the Blessed
in their heavenly glory have no need of the healing the Sacraments bestow. Joy without end is theirs, as in the presence
of God they gaze upon his glory, face to face; transfigured
from their own glory into that of the infinite Godhead, they
taste the Word of God become flesh, as he was from the
beginning and for ever remains.

3. When I recall these wonders to mind, I grow weary
even of spiritual consolation; for so long as I may not see
my Lord in his true glory, all that I see and hear in the
world means nothing to me. You are my witness, O my God,
that there is never a thing that can comfort me, never a
creature that can bring me rest, save only you, my God,
you upon whom I desire to gaze for ever. But this is not
possible in this mortal life, and so I must have great patience
and in all my desires submit myself to you. Those Saints of
yours, Lord, who now rejoice with you in the kingdom of
heaven, awaited the coming of your glory with faith and
much patience while they lived on earth. What they believed, I too believe; what they hoped for, I hope for too;
and through your grace I trust to come to that place where
they have already arrived. Till that happens, I will walk in

[1] 1 Cor. 13. 10.

202

faith, strengthened by the examples of the Saints. I shall also have holy books to comfort me and to mirror the life I would lead; above all, your most holy body shall be my particular remedy and refuge.

4. Now I am deeply conscious that there are two things necessary for me in this life; without them, this same life and all its sorrows would be more than I could bear. Pent in the prison of my body, I confess my need for two things, food and light. It is for this that you have given me in my weakness your holy body, to be a refreshment for soul and body; and you have set your word as a lamp to guide my feet. Without these two I could not properly live; the word of God is the light of my soul, and your Sacrament is the bread of life. You might even call them two tables, set one on this side, one on that, in the treasury of holy Church. One table is that of the holy altar; on it is the holy bread, the precious body of Christ. The other table is that of God's law, whereon is holy teaching, instructing us in the true faith and leading us without stumbling even beyond the veil hiding the Holy of Holies. I thank you, Lord Jesus, for the table of holy teaching, spread for us by means of your servants the prophets and apostles and other holy teachers.

5. O Creator and Redeemer of men, I thank you for shewing the whole world your love for men in preparing a great feast. Here it is no longer the lamb of ancient times that you have set before us to eat, but your own most holy body and blood. At this holy banquet you gladden the faithful, who drink brimming draughts from the cup of salvation, that cup wherein are all the delights of heaven; the angels, too, are our fellow guests, feasting with a joy even greater than ours.

6. How great and honourable is the office of those who are priests! They have been empowered to hallow with sacred words the Lord of majesty, to bless him with their lips, to hold him in their hands, to receive him with their own mouth and administer him to others. How frequently does the source of all purity enter into a priest! Then how

pure should those hands of his be, how holy his body, how free from stain his heart. From the mouth of a priest, who so often receives the Sacrament of Christ, no words should come forth but such as are holy, becoming and of benefit to others.

7. His eyes should be simple and chaste, for they often look upon the body of Christ, his hands pure and lifted up to heaven, for they often handle the Creator of heaven and earth. Priests in particular are addressed in those words of the Law, *You must be men set apart, as I am set apart, I, the Lord your God.*[1]

8. Almighty God, may we be helped by your grace; that we who have received the office of priesthood may be enabled to serve you worthily and devoutly in utter purity and with a good conscience. And if we cannot lead as sinless a life as we ought to, grant us nevertheless the grace to bewail the wrong we have done, and in the spirit of humility and with a resolve to choose the good, to serve you in future with greater fervour.

Chapter 12

ON THE GREAT CARE WE SHOULD TAKE IN PREPARING TO RECEIVE CHRIST IN HOLY COMMUNION

The Beloved: I am a lover of purity and the giver of all holiness. It is a pure heart that I look for; that is the place in which I rest. Make ready for me a large upper room, furnished; there will I and my disciples eat the Paschal meal with you. If you want me to come to you and remain with you, rid yourselves of the leaven which remains over and sweep clean the dwelling of your heart. Shut the door on the whole world and on the din of evil passions and sit there alone, like a single sparrow on the house top, thinking over your sins in the bitterness of your soul. Everyone who loves another makes ready for that beloved friend of his the best

[1] Lev. 19. 2.

and most beautiful room he has; in so doing he shews his loving joy at welcoming his friend to his home.

2. You must realize, though, that even were you to prepare for a whole year, with nothing else to give your mind to, you could make no adequate preparation for me, if I assessed your efforts by their merits. It is only through my kindness and grace that you are allowed access to my table; as if a beggar were invited to a rich man's dinner and were able to repay the kindness shewn him only by humbly expressing his thanks. Do the best you can, and do it with care, not from habit or necessity, but with loving dread and reverence receive the body of your beloved Lord and God, who lays aside his greatness to come to you. It is I who have invited you, I who have bidden this Sacrament to be; I will make up whatever in you is lacking; come and receive me.

3. When I accord you the grace of devout feelings, give thanks to your God for it, not that you deserve it, but because I have had pity upon you. If, on the other hand, you have no such feelings, but are conscious of dryness of heart, keep on with your prayers, knock at my door and sigh; never give up until you merit some crumb, some drop of my saving grace. You have need of me; I have no need of you. It is not you that come to make me holy; it is I that come to make you holier and better than before. You come to be made holy by me, to be made one with me; you come to receive fresh grace, to be fired anew with the desire to amend your life. Do not neglect this grace; make ready your heart with all the care you can, and then bring into it him whom you love.

4. You should not only make a devout preparation for Holy Communion, but keep yourself in that devout frame of mind when once you have received the Sacrament. Your watchful care after Communion is no less important than your devout preparation before it. When we keep good watch over ourselves after Communion, it is the best preparation we can make for receiving greater grace. For this we become ill-fitted indeed if we immediately rush off to the pleasures of

the visible world. Beware of much talking; stay by yourself in some place apart and there rejoice in the company of your God; there you have him within you, and the whole world cannot take him from you. I am he to whom you should surrender your whole being, so that henceforth, untouched by care, you may live no longer in yourself but in me.

Chapter 13

THE DEVOUT SOUL SHOULD LONG WITH HEARTFELT DESIRE FOR UNION WITH CHRIST IN THE BLESSED SACRAMENT

The Learner: If only, Lord, I might find you by yourself and lay bare to you all that is in my heart! Then I could enjoy your company, as my soul desires; then no one would scorn me, nothing created would trouble me or concern me; you alone would speak to me, as a lover does to his beloved, as a friend makes cheer with his friend. This is what I pray for, long for: to be made wholly one with you, to withdraw my heart from all created things, and through Holy Communion and frequent saying of Mass to learn more and more to delight in heavenly and eternal things. Ah, Lord God, when shall I be completely one with you, completely absorbed in you, utterly forgetful of myself? You in me and I in you; grant that we may remain in one for ever.

2. You are indeed *my sweetheart. Among ten thousand you shall know him;* in you my soul delights to make her home all the days of my life. You are he who brings me peace; in you is peace untroubled, rest unfeigned. Apart from you there is only toil and trouble and boundless grief. *Truly you are a God of hidden ways;*[1] no dealings do you have with the godless, but to lowly and simple folk you speak your heart. Lord, how sweet is your spirit! To shew your loving-kindness towards your children, you deign to refresh them with that most sweet bread that comes down from heaven. How true it is that *no other nation is so great; no other*

[1] Isa. 45. 15.

nation has gods that draw near to it, as our God draws near to[1] all his faithful. To comfort them every day, to raise their hearts daily to heaven, you give yourself to be their food and their delight.

3. What other people is so honoured as the Christian people? What creature under heaven is so beloved as a devout soul into whom God finds entrance, to nourish her with his glorious body? It is a grace that beggars speech, a stooping to our lowliness that fills us with wonder; a love beyond all measure, bestowed on mankind alone. But what return shall I make to the Lord for this grace, this love so high above other loves? No gift more welcome can I make him than to make over to him the whole of my heart, to be made one with his in the closest of unions. My whole inner being will be filled with joy when my soul is perfectly united to God. He will say to me then: "If you wish to be with me, I wish to be with you". And I shall answer him thus: "Stay with me, Lord, I beg you; willingly will I stay with you". This is the sum of my desires, that my heart should be united to you.

Chapter 14

ON THE BURNING DESIRE SOME DEVOUT PEOPLE HAVE FOR THE BODY OF CHRIST

The Learner: What treasures of loving kindness, Lord, do you store up for the men who fear you![2] Sometimes I think of those devout folk, Lord, who approach this Sacrament of yours with the utmost devotion and love; and many a time I blush for myself, feel guilty within me, to think that when I approach your altar, the table of your Holy Communion, I do so with my heart so cold and lacking in fervour. I am ashamed that I remain so dry, so void of love; that in your presence, my God, my heart does not burn within me, that I am not so strongly drawn and inwardly moved as I know many devout people have been. These, out of their

[1] Deut. 4. 8. [2] Ps. 30. 20.

overwhelming desire for Holy Communion, were powerless to keep back their tears, but from their inmost being yearned body and soul for you, my God, the living spring. In no other way could they abate or satisfy that hunger of theirs but by receiving your holy body with all joy and eagerness of soul.

2. How real that burning faith of theirs was, a living proof of the truth of your sacred presence! It is men such as these who truly know the Lord in the breaking of bread, men whose hearts burn so fiercely within them when Jesus walks at their side. For myself, I am often far from feeling such devotion and tenderness, so strong, so flaming a love. O good Jesus, so sweet, so kind, have pity on me; let me sometimes feel, poor penniless beggar that I am, at least something of that yearning for your love that stirs the heart. So will my faith grow stronger; so will my hope in your goodness be increased; and my love, once set wholly ablaze by the taste of this heavenly manna, will never fail.

3. Your mercy is powerful enough to grant me even this grace for which I long; to touch me, in your own good time, with the spirit of fervour. Even though I do not burn with that intense desire that fills the hearts of those utterly devoted to you, yet by your grace I desire to have that desire of theirs, that great, that flaming desire. For this do I yearn and pray, that I may join the ranks of all such ardent lovers of yours, take my place in their holy company.

Chapter 15

THE GRACE OF DEVOTION IS WON
BY HUMILITY AND SELF-DENIAL

The Beloved: You must ask for the grace of devotion with earnestness, must seek it with desire, wait for it with patience and confidence, welcome it with gratitude, keep it with humility, use it with care and leave to God the ending and the manner of this visit from on high until it comes again.

You should feel especially humble when you are conscious of little or no inward devotion, but not unduly depressed or unreasonably upset about it. God often gives you in a single short moment what he has withheld for a long time. Sometimes he gives you at last what he deferred giving when first you began praying for it.

2. If that grace were always given you at once, if you had only to pray for it to receive it, it would be more than man in his weakness could well endure. These devout feelings, therefore, with which God favours you, should be awaited with lively hope and unassuming patience. When it is not given to you, or even when you are conscious of its secret withdrawal, you must blame yourself and your sins for it. It is sometimes something very trivial which stands in the way of grace and conceals it; if anything can be called trivial, rather than serious, which acts as a barrier to so great a blessing. Once you have done away with this barrier, whether small or great, won a complete victory over it, what you pray for shall come to pass.

3. The moment you surrender yourself to God with all your heart, no longer seeking this or that as will or whim dictates, but placing yourself wholly in his charge, you will find yourself united to him, and your heart will be at peace; nothing will taste sweeter to you, nothing give you greater pleasure, than being obedient to the will of God. If a man, therefore, lifts up his intentions with unfeigning heart to God, making a clean sweep of any ill-regulated love or dislike for any creature, he will be fitly prepared to receive grace and worthy to be given the gift of devotion. It is when the Lord finds empty vessels that he fills them with his blessings. The more completely a man abjures the things of earth, the more he dies to himself by taking a low view of himself, the more speedy is the coming of grace, the more plentifully is it showered upon him, and the higher it lifts his unfettered heart.

4. Then shall he see; then shall the heart within him swell with wonder and overflow; for the hand of the Lord is upon him, and in that hand he has placed himself wholly

and for ever. This is the blessing that will come upon the man who seeks God whole-heartedly, the man who has not been given the gift of life in vain. When he receives the Holy Eucharist, he merits the great grace of union with God, for he is not concerned with his own devotion or comfort. Beyond all devotion and consolation, this is what he seeks: the honour and glory of God.

Chapter 16

WE SHOULD TELL CHRIST OUR NEEDS AND BEG FOR HIS GRACE

The Learner: O sweetest and most loving Lord, you whom I now long to receive devoutly, you know my weakness and the needs that I suffer; you know how many and great are the evils and the sinful tendencies that oppress me. You know how often I am heavy at heart, tempted to sin, troubled in mind and defiled in soul. It is to be cured that I come to you; it is for comfort and relief that I beseech you. He to whom I speak knows everything; yes, you can read my inmost thoughts, every one of them. It is you alone who can bring me perfect comfort, perfect help. You know what blessings I need before all others, you know how beggarly is my stock of virtues.

2. See, here I stand before you, naked and poor, begging for grace and imploring your pity. I am a beggar, and hungry; do you give me food. I am cold; warm me with the fire of your love. I am blind; enlighten my eyes with the brightness of your presence. Make all things on earth bitter to me, turn all affliction and trouble to patient acceptance; make me despise and forget all things below you, all things created. Lift up my heart to you in heaven; do not let me go, to be a wanderer over the face of the earth. Be my only delight, from now and for ever; you alone are my meat and drink, my love and my joy, my sweetness, my all-embracing good.

3. If only you would wholly enkindle me with the fire

of your presence, consume me with those flames, change me into yourself! So, by the grace of that inward union, that melting away beneath the heat of burning love, you and I would become a single spirit. Do not let me go from you hungry still and parched with thirst, but deal mercifully with me, as you have so often dealt in wonderful ways with your Saints. Small wonder it would be if I were wholly on fire with you, and myself dwindle to nothing; you are that fire that is ever blazing and never burning low, the love that cleanses the heart and brings light to the understanding.

Chapter 17

ON BURNING LOVE AND
EAGER LONGING TO RECEIVE CHRIST

The Learner: With all my devotion, Lord, with burning love, with all the fervent longing of my heart, I desire to receive you, as many Saints and devout folk have longed to receive you in Communion, people who were especially pleasing to you because their lives were holy, people in whom the fire of devotion blazed the highest. O my God, my everlasting love, my all-embracing good, my bliss without end, with irresistible longing I desire to receive you, with the fittest reverence that ever any Saint had or could feel.

2. Unworthy though I am to have such feelings of devotion as theirs, I offer you nonetheless my heart's whole love, as if I alone were filled by all those fiery longings of theirs for which I yearn so much. Nevertheless, whatever a devout soul can imagine or desire, that do I offer you, that do I make you a gift of, with the deepest reverence, the love of my inmost self. Nothing do I choose to keep back for myself, but freely and with all my heart I make an offering to you of myself and all that is mine. O Lord my God, my Creator, my Redeemer, I desire to receive you this day with affection, reverence, praise and honour, with that thankfulness, fitness and love, with that faith, hope and

purity with which your most holy Mother, the glorious Virgin Mary, desired and received you, when the Angel brought her the glad news of the mystery of the incarnation, and she in lowly reverence replied: *Behold the handmaid of the Lord; let it be unto me according to thy word.*[1]

3. Of old that blessed forerunner of yours, John the Baptist, highest among the Saints, filled with gladness at your presence, leaped for joy of the Holy Spirit while still in the shelter of his mother's womb. In after years, when he saw Jesus walking among men, in utter abasement he said with loving devotion: *The bridegroom's friend, who stands by and listens to him, rejoices too, rejoices at hearing the bridegroom's voice.*[2] So it is with me: I long to be afire with great and holy desires, and with all my heart to offer you myself. It is for this reason that I offer and lay before you the worship you receive from all devout hearts—their outbursts of joyous praise, their burning affection, their ecstasies, their spiritual insight, their heavenly visions; to these I add all the virtues, all the praises, that ever have been or will be offered to you in heaven or upon earth. I offer them for myself and for all for whom I have been asked to pray, that you may be given by all men that praise which is your due, and glory that has no end.

4. O Lord my God, accept these my prayers, this my desire that the praises men give you should have no limit, the times they bless you surpass all reckoning; for these are your lawful due, you whose greatness is such that it outsoars all human speech. So do I pray to you, so do I wish to pray each day, each moment of time; and with loving entreaty I beg and beseech all spirits in heaven and all your faithful on earth to join with me in giving you the praise and thanksgiving that are yours by right.

5. May all peoples, tribes and tongues give praise to you; may they extol that holy, that honey-sweet name of yours with cries of joyful praise and burning devotion; and may all who worshipfully and devoutly celebrate this great Sacrament of yours and receive it with unfailing faith,

[1] Luke 1. 38.   [2] John 3. 29.

212

deserve to find grace and mercy at your hands; and may they by their entreaties win your pardon for me and my sins; and when they have gained the devotion they hoped for, gained that union with yourself which is to bring them joy, and, greatly consoled and wonderfully refreshed, have left your sacred, your heavenly table, may they in kindness remember me and my poverty.

Chapter 18

A MAN SHOULD NOT SUBTLY PRY INTO THE BLESSED SACRAMENT, BUT FOLLOW CHRIST, SUBMITTING THE EVIDENCE OF HIS SENSES TO HOLY FAITH

The Beloved: If you have no wish to drown in the deep gulf of doubt, you must take care not to busy yourself with useless attempts to analyse this Sacrament, which goes deeper than human mind can fathom. *Search too high, and the brightness shall dazzle you.*[1] God's powers of action are greater than man's of comprehension. However, we may humbly and lovingly seek after truth, provided we are always ready to learn from others and strive to walk along those sound paths of opinion laid down by the Fathers.

2. He is a happy man who can simply turn aside from the uncharted ways of theological discussion and walk ahead by the sure and open road of God's commandments. There are many people who, in their desire to fathom mysteries too deep for them, have lost all feeling of devotion. What God wants of you is faith and a life of unalloyed goodness, not loftiness of understanding, not a probing of the deep mysteries of God. There are things beneath you which elude the grasp of your mind; how can you grasp those which are far above you? Submit yourself to God, humble the evidence of the senses before faith, and you will be given the light of knowledge in whatever measure is necessary for your spiritual welfare.

[1] Prov. 25. 27.

3. Many people have fierce temptations concerning faith and the Blessed Sacrament; this is not to be blamed on themselves, but rather on their enemy the Devil. Don't get worried about it, don't start arguing with these thoughts of yours, don't answer the doubts the Devil slips into your mind. Instead, put your faith in God's words, believe his Saints and prophets, and the wicked enemy will make off from you. It is often of great profit to a servant of God to have to bear with assaults of this kind. It is not sinners, not those without faith that the Devil tempts; they are his already, and he can afford not to worry about them. No, it is those who have the faith, those who are devout, whom he tempts and disquiets in many a way.

4. Go forward, then, with simple, unfaltering faith, and approach the Sacrament in unquestioning adoration. Leave your worries behind and entrust to almighty God whatever is beyond the grasp of your understanding. God never misleads you; a man may well mislead himself when he puts too much faith in his own powers. It is with simple folk that God walks, to the humble that he makes himself known; to little ones he gives understanding, to the pure of heart he rends the veil of outward appearance. From those who in their arrogance pry into his secrets he hides his grace. Human reason is weak and may be mistaken; there is no making mistakes for true faith.

5. All reason and natural enquiry must follow faith, not precede it or trespass on its domain. Here, in the most holy, the most sublime of the Sacraments, faith and love are paramount, causing their effects in ways beyond man's knowing. God, who is outside your time, outside your human ways of measuring things, brings about by his limitless power great and unsearchable things in heaven and earth; you cannot track those wonders of his to their author. If the works of God came easily within the grasp of human reason, there would be nothing in them to wonder at, nothing to make you say they transcended human speech.

INDEX

Adversity, the uses of, 30-1, 37, 129; to be borne patiently, 102, 111-2, 136-7; the example of Christ, 110. *See* Cross

Advice, better to receive than to give, 26; value of good advice, 23, 32, 95, 199

Agatha, St, 148

Ambition, 68, 121

Amendment of life, 56-9

Apostles, their example, 38, 118

Avarice, 23-4

Bethany, 134

Books, which to be read and how, 23; the Scriptures especially necessary for us, 201-2

Cares, to be cast on God, 109-10; freedom from, 123-4

Cell, to be frequented, 44-5

Christ, *see* Jesus Christ

Communion, *see* Holy Communion

Confession, 93, 188, 200

Conscience, joy of a good, 43, 67-8

Consolation and Desolation, 72-4, 84-6, 87, 93, 95, 103, 108-9, 162

Contempt of self, 19; of pleasures and honours, 62, 132, 143. *See* Humility

Contrition, 17, 44, 45-6, 163

Conversation, with God, 60-3, 70-2; with men, 25, 43-4, 64-5, 193

Courage, 172

Cross of Jesus, to be loved and carried with patience and joy, 76-7, 171-2

Curiosity, about the affairs of others, 121; about difficult matters, 146, 174-8, 213-4

David, King, his devotion, 183

Death, the thought of, 50-3

Defects, our own to be considered rather than those of others, 36-7, 66

Desolation, 72-4, 116, 123, 158-61

Detachment from creatures, 130-2, 164

Devil, 93, 103, 199

Devotion, prayer for, 88; to be concealed, 94-6; towards the Eucharist, 207, 211-2

Enlightening of the mind, prayer for, 120

Eternity, the day of, 153-4; desire of, 155-6

Eucharist, the Holy, *see* Holy Communion *and* Mass

Examination of conscience, 41, 194-5

Example of Christ, 104, 110; of the Saints, 38-9, 176; of good men, 57

External things, how to be used, 139, 146-7

Familiarity, excessive, to be avoided, 25-6

Fervour, 56-9

Francis of Assisi, St, 161

Friendship with Jesus, to be sought above all, 69-72, 121, 164, 179

God, our final end, 98, 134-5; without him we are nothing, 105-6, 130, 141-2; our peace and comfort, 108-9, 114-5, 128-9, 134-5, 160; all our trust to be placed in him, 178-80

Grace, 75-6; to be guarded by humility, 94-5; not given to worldlings, 164-5; contrasted with nature, 165-8

Heaven, the glory of, 54-5, 87, 93, 152, 153, 154, 155-8, 176, 202

Hell, 47, 54-6, 102, 163

Holy Communion, 93; the sacrament of love, 186-7; to be received reverently, 181-5, and with due preparation, 185, 194-6, 204-5; most necessary for the soul, 201-4; the fruit of devout and frequent reception, 184-5, 188-9, 199-200; thanksgiving after, 205-6; to be regarded with desire and devotion, 206-8

Honours, not to be sought, 143

Hope, to be placed in God, 24-5, 155

Humility, 18-9, 23, 63, 88, 94-7 98, 105-6, 113, 118, 144, 161 163, 177-8, 208-9

Idleness, 41

Inconstancy of heart, 133-4

Injuries, to be borne patiently, 111-2, 137-8, 149-50

Jesus Christ, to be followed as our leader and example, 1 and *passim*; with a union of friendship and love, 60-3, 69-70, 90-4; his cross to be carried by us, 76-83; speaks inwardly to the soul, 84-6; his humility 104, and patience under suffering, 93, 110; our consoler, 108, and

Jesus Christ, *continued*
the source of rest, 117-8; his love in the Blessed Sacrament, 181*ff*.

Joshua, 140

Judgement, day of, 21, 53-5

Judgements, the secret judgements of God, 105, 174-8; the rash judgements of men, 34, 137-8

Knowledge, can be vain and harmful, 18-22, 145-6

Labour, value of, 151-2

Learning, true and false, 18-23, 131, 145-6

Love, of God, 35, 69-70; self-denial a proof of love, 76-83, 92-4; the wonderful effects of love, 90-92; love of God impaired by self-love, 124-5, and by the love of creatures, 84; love of friends, 144, 164; love of our neighbour, 25-6, 35-7, 98

Lukewarmness, 29, 66, 111, 195

Man, has no good of himself, 141-3; is not to be trusted, 148-9

Mary, Mother of God, 187, 212. *See* Our Lady

Mass, Holy, 185, 187, 196-8, 201

Miracles of Christ, 111

Misery, human, 47-50, 110-1, 113-4

Monastic life, 37-42, 56-9, 99-100

Mortification, 37, 76-83. *See* Self-denial

Moses, 85, 140, 182

Nature, contrasted with Grace, 165-8

Noe and his ark, 182

Obedience, 26-7, 37-8, 104-5

Our Lady, 187, 212

Passion of Christ, 61, 80, 93

Passions, immoderate, 23, 65, 101-2, 131, 164; not to be followed but checked, 23-4, 29, 57; passion not to be mistaken for zeal, 66

Patience, 102, 111-2, 136-7; of Christ, 110

Peace of mind, 28, 86, 107, 122-3, 143

Peaceable man, the, 64-9

Perseverance, 56, 172, 174

Pilgrimages, 51, 184

Pilgrims and strangers, 37, 52-3

Poverty, religious, 23, 38

Pride, 24-5, 95, 104, 106

Priesthood, the, 192-3, 201, 203-4

Prudence, 22, 95

Purgatory, 47, 53, 102

Purity of heart, 65-6, 71, 139, 204

Recollection, 107

Resignation, 107, 109, 138-9

Saints, their inspiring examples, 38, 93, 94, 152, 153; we should not dispute about their relative merits, 174-8

Samuel, 85

Scriptures, the Holy, how to be read, 23; a source of comfort, 162, and very necessary for us, 201-4

Self-criticism, 66-7

Self-denial, 76-83, 132-3, 138-9, 141, 171-2, 209

Service of God, a privilege and a joy, 99-100

Sickness, few men improved by, 51

Silence, 27, 42-5

Simplicity of heart, 65-6, 88

Slanderers, 126, 149-51

Solitude, 42-4, 164

Solomon, 182

Sorrow for sin, 17, 44-5, 46-7, 163

Submissiveness, 26-7, 63, 157

Suffering, value of, 53, 61, 63. *See* Cross

Talking, 27, 42-5

Temporal things, full of vanity, 84, 108, 140, 143

Temptations, 31-3, 87, 93, 94, 136-7

Thanksgiving, 75-6, 99-100, 117-8, 205

Travel, does not sanctify, 51

Trials and tribulations, 31-3, 61-2, 81-2, 96, 110, 111-2, 127, 136-7, 151-2, 153, 158-9, 171-4

Truth, speaks inwardly to us, 84-6; walking in truth, 88-90; to be sought with humility, 213-4

Union with God, 60-3, 185-92

Vainglory, 98, 105-6, 143

Vanity of vanities, 18, 24-5

Vestments, 193

Vision, the Beatific, 153-4, 202

Will of God, prayer for its fulfilment in us, 107-8; should be our joy, 118

Wisdom, prayer for, 125-6

Words of God, 85-6

Work, our daily, 35-6, 41, 103, 152

Worldliness, 86-7, 102-3, 114, 124, 135

Zaccheus, 188

Zeal, to be directed against ourselves, 64; passion not to be mistaken for it, 66